DEMOCRACY AND CIVIL SOCIETY IN EASTERN EUROPE

SELECTED PAPERS FROM THE FOURTH WORLD CONGRESS FOR SOVIET AND EAST EUROPEAN STUDIES, HARROGATE, 1990

Edited for the International Council for Soviet and East European Studies by Stephen White, Professor of Politics, University of Glasgow

From the same publishers:

Roy Allison (*editor*)
RADICAL REFORM IN SOVIET DEFENCE POLICY

Ben Eklof (*editor*)
SCHOOL AND SOCIETY IN TSARIST AND SOVIET RUSSIA

John Elsworth (*editor*)
THE SILVER AgE IN RUSSIAN LITERATURE

John Garrard and Carol Garrard (*editors*)
WORLD WAR 2 AND THE SOVIET PEOPLE

Zvi Gitelman (*editor*)
THE POLITICS OF NATIONALITY AND THE EROSION OF THE USSR

Sheelagh Duffin Graham (*editor*)
NEW DIRECTIONS IN SOVIET LITERATURE

Celia Hawkesworth (*editor*)
LITERATURE AND POLITICS IN EASTERN EUROPE

Lindsey Hughes (*editor*)
NEW PERSPECTIVES ON MUSCOVITE HISTORY

Walter Joyce (*editor*)
SOCIAL CHANGE AND SOCIAL ISSUES IN THE FORMER USSR

Bohdan Krawchenko (*editor*)
UKRAINIAN PAST, UKRAINIAN PRESENT

Paul G. Lewis (*editor*)
DEMOCRACY AND CIVIL SOCIETY IN EASTERN EUROPE

Robert B. McKean (*editor*)
NEW PERSPECTIVES IN MODERN RUSSIAN HISTORY

John Morison (*editor*)
THE CZECH AND SLOVAK EXPERIENCE
EASTERN EUROPE AND THE WEST

John O. Norman (*editor*)
NEW PERSPECTIVES ON RUSSIAN AND SOVIET ARTISTIC CULTURE

Derek Offord (*editor*)
THE GOLDEN AGE OF RUSSIAN LITERATURE AND THOUGHT

Michael E. Urban (*editor*)
IDEOLOGY AND SYSTEM CHANGE IN THE USSR AND EAST EUROPE

Democracy and Civil Society in Eastern Europe

Selected Papers from the Fourth World Congress for Soviet and East European Studies, Harrogate, 1990

Edited by

Paul G. Lewis
Senior Lecturer in Government
The Open University

First published in Great Britain 1992 by
THE MACMILLAN PRESS LTD
Houndmills, Basingstoke, Hampshire RG21 2XS
and London
Companies and representatives throughout the world

This book is published in association with the International Council for Soviet and
East European Studies.

A catalogue record for this book is available from the British Library

ISBN 0–333–56776–5

Printed and bound in Great Britain by
Antony Rowe Ltd, Chippenham, Wiltshire

First published in the United States of America 1992 by
Scholarly and Reference Division,
ST. MARTIN'S PRESS, INC.,
175 Fifth Avenue,
New York, N.Y. 10010

ISBN 0–312–08042–5

Library of Congress Cataloging-in-Publication Data
World Congress for Soviet and East European Studies (4th : 1990 :
Harrogate, England)
Democracy and civil society in eastern Europe : selected papers
from the fourth World Congress for Soviet and East European Studies,
Harrogate, 1990 / edited by Paul G. Lewis.
p. cm.
Includes index.
ISBN 0–312–08042–5
1. Civil society—Europe, Eastern —Congresses. 2. Post-communism-
-Europe, Eastern—Congresses. 3. Europe, Eastern—Politics and
government—1989- —Congresses. 4. Europe, Eastern—Social
conditions—Congresses. I. Lewis, Paul G., 1945- .
II. International Council for Soviet and East European Studies.
III. Title.
JC599.E92W67 1992
306.2'0947—dc20
                                                    92–1049
                                                      CIP

10 9   8   7   6   5   4   3
03 02 01 00 99 98 97 96

Contents

General Editor's Introduction

The Fourth World Congress for Soviet and East European Studies took place in Harrogate, Yorkshire, in July 1990. It was an unusual congress in many ways. It was the first of its kind to take place in Britain, and the first to take place since the launching of Gorbachev's programme of *perestroika* and the revolutions in Eastern Europe (indeed so rapid was the pace of change in the countries with which we were concerned that the final programme had to incorporate over 600 amendments). It was the largest and most complex congress of Soviet and East European studies that has yet taken place, with twenty-seven panels spread over fourteen sessions on six days. It was also the most representative congress of its kind, with over 2000 participants including – for the first time – about 300 from the USSR and Eastern Europe. Most were scholars, some were activists, and a few were the new kind of academic turned part-time deputy: whatever their status, it was probably this Soviet and East European presence that contributed most directly to making this a very different congress from the ones that had preceded it in the 1970s and 1980s.

No series of volumes, however numerous, could hope to convey the full flavour of this extraordinary occasion. The formal panels alone incorporated almost a thousand papers. There were three further plenary sessions; there were many more unattached papers; and the subjects that were treated ranged from medieval Novgorod to computational linguistics, from the problems of the handicapped in the USSR to Serbian art at the time of the battle of Kosovo. Nor, it was decided at an early stage, would it even be desirable to attempt a fully comprehensive 'congress proceedings', including all the papers in their original form. My aim as General Editor, with the strong support of the International Council for Soviet and East European Studies (who cosponsored the congress with the British Association for Soviet, Slavonic and East European Studies), has rather been to generate a series of volumes which will have some thematic coherence, and to bring them out as quickly as possible while their (often topical) contents are still current.

A strategy of this kind imposes a cost, in that many authors have had to find other outlets for what would in different circumstances have been very publishable papers. The gain, however, seems much greater: a series of real books on properly defined subjects, edited by scholars of experience and standing in their respective fields, and placed promptly before the academic community. These, I am glad to say, were the same as the objectives of the publishers who expressed an interest in various aspects of the congress proceedings, and it has led to a series of volumes as well as of special issues of journals covering a wide range of interests. There are volumes on art and architecture, on history and literature, on law and economics, on society and education. There are further volumes on nationality issues and the Ukraine, on the environment, on international relations and on defence. There are Soviet volumes, and others that deal more specifically with Eastern (or, perhaps more properly, East Central) Europe. There are interdisciplinary volumes on women in Russia and the USSR, the Soviet experience in the Second World War, and ideology and system change. There are special issues of some of the journals that publish in our field, dealing with religion and Slovene studies, émigrés and East European economics, publishing and politics, linguistics and the Russian revolution. Altogether nearly forty separate publications will stem from the Harrogate congress: more than twice as many as from any previous congress of its kind, and a rich and enduring record of its deliberations.

Most of these volumes will be published in the United Kingdom by Macmillan. It is my pleasant duty to acknowledge Macmillan's early interest in the scholarly output of the congress, and the swift and professional attention that has been given to all of these volumes since their inception. A full list of the Harrogate series appears in the Macmillan edition of this volume; it can give only an impression of the commitment and support I have enjoyed from Tim Farmiloe, Clare Wace and others at all stages of our proceedings. I should also take this opportunity to thank John Morison and his colleagues on the International Council for Soviet and East European Studies for entrusting me with this responsible task in the first place, and the various sponsors – the Erasmus Prize Fund of Amsterdam, the Ford Foundation in New York, the British Foreign and Commonwealth Office, the British Council, the Stefan Batory Trust and others – whose generous support helped to make the congress a reality.

The next congress will be held in 1995, and (it is hoped) at a location in Eastern Europe. Its proceedings can hardly hope to improve upon the vigour and imagination that is so abundantly displayed on the pages of these splendid volumes.

University of Glasgow   STEPHEN WHITE

Notes on the Contributors

Irene Dölling is Director of the Institut für Kulturwissenschaft at Humbold University in Berlin, having acted as the first head of the Centre for Interdisciplinary Women's Studies there from 1989. Her publications have been in the area of cultural theory, gender relations and personality development, and current research concerns sociocultural change in everyday German life following unification.

Chris Hann is Professor of Social Anthropology at the University of Kent and previously lectured at Cambridge University. His main publications have been *Tazlar: a Village in Hungary* (1980), *A Village without Solidarity: Polish Peasants in Years of Crisis* (1985) and, as editor, *Market Economy and Civil Society in Hungary* (1990). He is currently preparing a general book on 'The Anthropology of Eastern Europe'.

Tomasz Goban-Klas and **Teresa Sasinska-Klas** are, respectively, Professor of Sociology and Adjunct Professor at the Institute of Political Science in Cracow, specialising in the areas of communication and journalism. They have published, mostly in Polish, on communication theory and the media, political communication and socialisation, and youth culture.

Ágnes Horváth and **Árpád Szakolczai** are research fellows in the Institute of Sociology at the Hungarian Academy of Sciences. They have published, respectively, on contemporary Western social theory and the history of economic and political thought. Szakolczai has more recently been Lecturer at the European University Institute, Florence. Their book on *The Dissolution of Communist Power in Hungary*, which extends themes introduced in their contribution to this book, is forthcoming.

Knud Erik Jørgensen is research fellow at the Institute of Political Science, University of Aarhus, and is associated with the Centre for Peace and Conflict Research at the University of Copenhagen, whose financial support he acknowledges in the preparation of this chapter. He has published works on the Polish opposition, Western responses to Soviet policy under Gorbachev and issues of European security.

Paul G. Lewis is Senior Lecturer in Government at the Open University. He has published in the areas of comparative and international politics, and the politics and sociology of Eastern Europe with particular reference to Poland. He is currently preparing 'A History of Central Europe since 1945' and is engaged on a collaborative research project on regime change in East-Central Europe, funded by the Economic and Social Research Council.

Tomaž Mastnak is a Senior Research Fellow at the Institute of Philosophy in the Centre of Scientific Research, the Slovene Academy of Sciences and Arts, Ljubljana. His works include *Towards a Critique of Stalinism*, and he has edited *A Socialist Civil Society?* and *Two Centuries of the Disputability of Revolution*. His current research is into early eighteenth-century English political thought.

Witold Morawski is Professor of Sociology at the University of Warsaw, having spent the year 1990–1 as visiting professor at the University of Toronto. He has published widely on questions of economic organisation, management and industrial relations and general issues of economy and society. He is joint editor of a recent book on basic problems of sociology and is currently conducting research into the transition to democracy and the market.

Melanie Tatur works at the Forschungstelle Osteuropa, University of Bremen, and from 1991 also (with a newly established team) studies the Soviet Union at the Institute of Political Studies of the Polish Academy of Sciences. Her main research interests concern the industrial and political sociology of Eastern Europe and the Soviet Union, while her publications have dealt with the Solidarity movement and the working class in Poland.

Jacek Wasilewski is an Associate Professor at the Institute of Sociology, University of Cracow, and heads the elite studies section of the Institute of Political Studies at the Polish Academy of Sciences. Recent publications concern elites and patterns of elite recruitment and contemporary developments in the Polish parliament, in both of which areas he is also conducting further research.

Introduction
Paul G. Lewis

The end of the Cold War and the abrupt lifting of the Iron Curtain in
Europe during 1989 brought into focus for the first time since shortly
after the Second World War real prospects for the establishment of
democracy in Eastern Europe. Exactly 200 years after the upheavals of
the French Revolution, which placed the idea of popular sovereignty
and mass democracy firmly on the political agenda, the defeat of
absolutism in Western Europe was commemorated by a similar dismantling of communist dictatorship in the east of the continent.
However the progress of democratisation since the late eighteenth
century has not run an even course. It has come in several waves, the
timing of them varying slightly according to the account given by
different writers. For Robert Dahl the key periods have been 1776–
1930, 1950–9 and the 1980s.[1] Huntington refers to the period from the
1820s to the post-First World War years, 1945–60, and from 1974 (with
the end of the Greek and Portuguese dictatorships) to the 1980s.[2] The
involvement of Eastern Europe in the most recent wave of democratisation reflected developments that were rapid and unexpected, as well as
carrying implications that were highly significant for the nature of the
post war global order and even certain aspects of the character of
political life in the modern world.[3]

For Dahl, in a work published as the first East European communist
dictatorships were already crumbling, the end of the dictatorial order in
Eastern Europe appeared to be a distant prospect, although this was less
a judgement based on domestic conditions than one premised on Soviet
post war dominance and the relations that prevailed in the region right
up to 1989.[4] The demise of communist dictatorship in Eastern Europe
had considerable significance and carried major implications in a
variety of areas. Unlike many of the recently formed democracies (in
Southern Europe and Latin America, for example) those seeking to
become established in Eastern Europe did not generally appear as
examples of redemocratisation and were building on a fairly tenuous
historical base of political democracy (Czechoslovakia here being a
notable exception). Neither did they form, at least in the more specific
sense, part of a process of decolonialisation but represented the
democratisation of relatively advanced, modern societies.

While it would not be accurate to state that emancipation was

1

achieved solely by autonomous national action (while under contemporary conditions democratisation must in any case be seen as part of a largely transnational process or processes), the East European developments did represent a decisive rejection of communist dictatorship and threw new light on the nature, strength and staying power of modern totalitarianism, hitherto often regarded as a virtually irresistible threat to democracy. Finally they seemed to carry new implications for the nature and role of the modern state in relation to contemporary forms of civil society as they had developed within the communist system. Civil society suddenly seemed stronger and more prominent within the context of modern life than anyone had foreseen, and its role in eroding dictatorship and facilitating the establishment of democracy correspondingly more powerful and direct. The establishment and prospective consolidation of democracy on the basis of less constrained economic processes and a strengthened civil society is, indeed, seen as a major political aspect of the current changes in Eastern Europe.

Democracy in the early stages of post-communist development has primarily been understood in terms of the further enhancement of social autonomy and the strengthening of its association with forces which have pushed back and superseded the state-centred dictatorship of the communist system. Political democracy has been closely linked with the encouragement of market economics and the retreat of the state from the administration of economic processes; liberalism and the principles of free association have taken over from state organisation and the bureaucratic co-ordination of social life. The development of capitalist, market economies has been formally endorsed as a precondition for and concomitant of the development of political democracy. The Conference on Security and Co-operation in Europe, which ended in April 1990, formally recognised in its concluding document the relationship between political pluralism and market economics and emphasised that political pluralism was essential for the sustenance of economic development, while economic well-being itself was best achieved through the operation of market forces.

Capitalism and democracy have therefore been identified as joint partners in the creation of the post-communist future. Open economies have been associated not merely with the development of free polities but also with the restructuring of state–society relations and a classic liberal emphasis on the reduction of state powers. But it is too simple a representation to portray recent changes just as the decline of an inclusive, totalitarian state power in the face of a civil society which embodies all the forces of freedom and democracy. As well as emphatic endorsement such views have also attracted trenchant criticism, in one case being described as misconceived and the utopian elements contained in them 'naive and dangerous'.[5] The rush to encapsulate the on-going changes in Eastern Europe in a new cluster of concepts whose relations with one another have yet to be fully thought out is open to critical examination from a number of angles.

Totalitarianism, firstly, involved only in a loose sense the repression of society and civic institutions by state agencies. State institutions and government bodies were caught up and used in the totalitarian drive against society but, it may be argued, the offices and organisations of state were used by totalitarianism rather than embodying its essence, and state as much as society was its victim in Eastern Europe. To describe totalitarianism in terms of the increasing encroachment of the state on society, in one view, is to miss the point of what happened in Nazi Germany or Stalin's Russia in terms of the state and its institutions. Leonard Schapiro argued that totalitarianism, embodied in the person of the leader and his apparatus of control, ate its way into the fabric 'of *both* state *and* society'.[6] It was here that the real nature of the "totalitarian" regime was revealed.' Civil society, as these remarks suggest, is by no means antithetical to the idea of the state and exercise of its authority – although civil society is usually now defined as in opposition to its structures.

Views and evidence from different parts of the world suggest, indeed, that the scope of civil society may extend in concert with growth in the power of the state, although there is certainly no direct one-to-one relationship and the complexity of state–civil society relations needs fully to be taken into account. This has been confirmed on one analysis which concerned regimes very different in terms of background and social dynamics from those of Eastern Europe but not dissimilar in terms of some of the challenges and systemic problems they faced. They were regimes in Latin America 'currently beset both by problems of political legitimacy and by an apparent inability to deal with the international economic context of the 1980s', difficulties which 'stimulated new interest in the interaction between civil society and the state in authoritarian contexts'.[7] Vigorous and specifically political initiatives have been identified as necessary for the 'survival and expansion of civil society' while, in similar fashion, sovereign state power is an 'indispensable condition of the democratisation of civil society'.[8]

But current conceptions, including those commonly applied to contemporary Eastern Europe, often tend to treat civil society in a negative sense as the 'realm of social relations not regulated by the state', which means that it is not possible to fix the meaning and extension of the term without doing the same for the state itself.[9] A more considered view suggests rather that civil society is 'located outside, though not disconnected from, the institutional framework of the state'.[10] The precise relationship of the state with civil society remains a matter of some debate both empirically and in normative terms. The exaggeration of the distinctiveness of civil society and the state to the extent that their development and the kind of values they embody might be regarded as mutually contradictory was a tendency that gained strength during the 1980s, but one conditioned more by the resurgence of liberal principles in the West and the reorientation of its economic principles than by insight into the conditions developing in Eastern Europe or consideration of the changing parameters of social and political life there.

Nor are the interests of democracy by any means best served by discounting the role of the state or minimising the conditions of its development. Ironically both the strong links rapidly forged between civic freedom, democracy and the capitalist market following the collapse of communism throughout much of Eastern Europe and the limited value placed on state action recall the highly specific and restricted conceptions both of civil society and the state found in the Marxian account. While the state, for Marx, was often regarded as nothing more than the instrument of bourgeois dominance, so civil society was the realm of commodity production and exchange – but this contained little of the social autonomy and civic freedom now foreseen and whose development is desired in the wake of the communist dictatorships and the social deformations they caused. The idea of civil society has, indeed, been subject to considerable variation and used (or, it might be added, abused) in a variety of contexts. Few social and political concepts, notes Zbigniew Pelczynski, have 'travelled so far in their life and changed their meaning so much'.[11]

The origins of the term are at least clear; well into the eighteenth century no distinction was made between the idea of a civil society and that of the state: the member of a civil society was at the same time a citizen subject to the laws of political community and bound to act in accordance with its prescriptions. Judgements on later connotations of the term, the shifts in meaning they implied and the sharpness of the distinctions reflected do, however, differ somewhat. Keane places considerable emphasis on the changes in usage that occurred during the second half of the eighteenth century as the intellectual landscape of the early modern world underwent fundamental transformation and the democratic revolution gathered pace, erupting first in North America and then in France.[12] The changes were, however, more marked in some *milieux* and countries than others, a factor further contributing to the variations in usage and continuing to mark the cultural understandings within which contemporary discussion is conducted.

The Scottish philosopher, Ferguson, for example, discussed relations between civil society and the threat of political despotism, preparing the ground for the subsequent examination of tensions between civil society and the state. This theme was further developed by Thomas Paine, with his emphasis on the value and empirical possibility of a naturally self-regulating society and the conditional rights of the formally constituted state. Hegel, on the other hand, saw civil society as standing in a more intimate relationship with, and in closer need of, regulation and surveillance by, the state – which thereby represented the immanent unity of society and transcended the conflicts with which it was riven. Marx's conception, while clearly different in orientation and conclusion, reflected the structure of Hegel's vision and also saw civil society as productive of contradiction and conflict, an entity to be transcended and reproduced at a higher level of social development. The status and role of civil society as a central component of the societal whole were thus becoming steadily reduced by the middle of the nineteenth century.

Within the discourse of the Left, Marx's restrictive definition of civil society thus gave little scope for it to emerge as a significant actor in the class-dominated conflicts of the modern period or to receive much in the way of theoretical attention. It did receive considerable emphasis in the writings of Antonio Gramsci, although it had been argued that his extensive use of the civil society concept is precisely what distinguishes him from the mainstream Marxist tradition.[13] For the Right, civil society provided little guidance to the formations of the modern period and acted more as a reference back to a situation that prevailed before the advent of mass urban–industrial society. Nevertheless it remained available and relevant to thinkers in the liberal tradition as a relatively old-fashioned term identifying an 'aggregate of institutions whose members are engaged primarily in a complex of non-state activities – economic and cultural production, household life and voluntary institutions – and who in this way preserve and transform their identity by exercising all sorts of pressures or controls upon state institutions'.[14]

Under contemporary conditions, however, many held that the idea of a civil society independent of the state had little relevance with the passing of the early phase of modernity marked by features of a classic liberalism. It was, then, paradoxical that it was developments of

Eastern Europe, where elements of a liberal heritage and the forms of liberal democracy were even weaker, that placed the idea of civil society once more at the forefront of the contemporary political agenda. To the extent that the term did have any prominence prior to these developments, it was to the developed Western countries that it was conventionally applied. Yet it was in the face of the apparently strongest and most tightly organised form of state power, totalitarian dictatorship, that civil society increased its resources and seemed to grow in stature sufficiently to pose a critical challenge to the exercise and very existence of that dictatorship. It is, however, important not to exaggerate the role and strength of civil society in Eastern Europe. It is too easy, in retrospect, to interpret all signs of opposition to communist rule and the series of examples of regime instability as signs of the growth and progressive development of an East European civil society.

Such an interpretation would neglect the fact that all the early crises of communist rule in Eastern Europe reflected significant, and sometimes dominant, features of division and conflict within the elite.[15] While this could hardly fail to be the case within the centralised systems of communist Eastern Europe, the elite dimension often dominated to the extent that the element of popular mobilisation clearly played a subsidiary role and any notion of civil society was a very distant prospect. Where mass involvement and popular mobilisation did develop to a high level, as in Hungary during 1956, it was more appropriate to ascribe the passion and commitment that was evident to sentiments of resurgent nationalism, rather than to the notions of interest and pressure associated with the steady growth of civil society and its influence. Nationality had tended to be regarded in the nineteenth century as a social characteristic superseded by the development of civil society, although its role in modern societies retained considerable ambiguity.[16] But it was also possible, as early as 1956 in Hungary and Poland, to identify tendencies to self-organisation within the broad currents of opposition that did indeed point to the development and potential existence of a civil society in Eastern Europe.

It took a considerable period of time for that potential to become more real, and then a specific set of conditions were necessary for the development to occur. Two were particularly important. The more relaxed style of political rule in Hungary and Poland during the 1970s (although with state repression still available and frequently used on a selective basis) provided more favourable conditions for social organisation and the development of shared interests. Important here were the atmosphere of detente, strengthened ties with the Western powers (particularly in the economic sphere) and greater use of the language of human rights, whose suggestion of an equivalence between East and West (however superficial in practice) nevertheless provided an important symbolic basis for the growth of tendencies pointing to the development of a civil society. A second factor was the exhaustion of all hopes of reform and effective development, particularly in Poland, from within the communist establishment and, more specifically, the party elite.

The events of 1968, which involved a comprehensive purge of revisionists and prominent Jewish intellectuals, were a major landmark in this process, while the fate of demonstrators and strikers during 1970 in Gdańsk, Szczeciń and elsewhere showed once more the weakness and vulnerability of isolated workers' opposition. It was only after further violence during 1976 (mainly in Radom and Ursus), however, that intellectuals and middle-class opposition representatives grew closer to the workers' movement and laid the foundations for a broader network that could be seen to have some links with the prospect of a civil society. It is important to recognise that this development grew out of a specific phase of political disenchantment, took form under particular political conditions and represented the espousal of a distinctive political strategy rather than the growth of a more general social identity. It might, therefore, be more appropriate to describe the spread of a democratic opposition and dissident movement in Poland towards the end of the 1970s in Tocquevillean terms as the rebirth of a *political* society rather than one representing the more general reality of a civil society.[17]

It is also important to recognise that these developments, the earliest and most important forerunners of and pointers to the development of a civil society, were given organisational form and led by a small group of political activists some of whom had previously been associated with reformist currents in the political establishment but who, at the same time as political conditions gave some scope for unorthodox and critical activity, now turned away from all ideas of achieving change through the established structures of communist party and state. Committing themselves to the defence of persecuted workers in 1976 as the Committee for Workers' Defence (KOR) they began to forge links (on a very small scale) with sections of the working class and on this basis to form the embryo of an alternative political network more representative of society as a whole. Accompanying the change was a new approach towards the Catholic Church. The resignation from all hopes of change in the communist establishment prompted the highly significant and (from his standpoint) surprising insight of Adam Michnik, expressed in the mid-1970s, that it was the Catholic Church in Poland which remained a 'key source of encouragement for those who seek to broaden civil liberties'.[18]

This was an important new element in strategies of social change in Eastern Europe and, more than any other single factor in the sequence of developments prior to the fall of Gierek (especially if it is associated with an unexpected but related external development: the election of a Polish pope), provided a crucial symbolic basis for the development of Solidarity as a social movement. The combination of a new strategy of social change with an intellectual rationale which permitted a direct rapport with the core religious and national values of Polish society (no full separation of the two elements was possible in cultural terms) facilitated in 1980 the explosive expansion of the numerically limited collaboration of intellectuals and workers that had been established in 1976. It was this, more than any other factor, which made possible observations on the distinctive character in Eastern Europe of the constitution of a civil society from below and the rise of a social movement consciously espousing its values.[19]

The rise of the Solidarity movement was of critical importance in demonstrating in concrete terms the social resources in Eastern Europe that could be mobilised against the communist establishment and its dictatorial state, as well as bringing back to theoretical prominence the prospect of civil society. Yet the resurgent society was unable to maintain the gains made in 1980 and both it and Solidarity were once more pushed underground by martial law. Writing after 1989, it is difficult not to see the return of both to the surface as only a matter of time, although this outcome was by no means so certain following the reassertion of communist power and in view of the unpromising prospects for democratic reform throughout the region with the minimal pace of change in the Soviet Union during the 1980s. The military response to Solidarity and the challenge of Polish civil society nevertheless did perform a positive function. Communist power in Poland had little hope of becoming invisible, as it could pretend to be in 'normalised' Czechoslovakia.

The experience both of Solidarity and its militarised repression made the roots of communist power visible once more and did away with what Melucci calls the 'show-business' aspects of politics (a perception brilliantly seized and played upon by 'Major' Frydrych with his Orange Alternative and surrealist street-theatre).[20] The future of civil society and a democratic outcome in Eastern Europe after Solidarity was by no means assured, but neither did it appear credible that the contradictions between society and communist state (most noticeable in Hungary amongst the other countries of Eastern Europe) would be effectively overcome or that the system would be capable of long-term survival. The events of 1989 settled most doubts on that score but raised others of a more theoretical and long-term nature. Most pressing was (and is) the question of whether the conditions and combination of forces that led to the collapse of communist dictatorship were sufficient and comprehensive enough to sustain the more constructive process of democratisation.

In this discussion the role and nature of civil society in Eastern Europe must take pride of place, and the question is one to which the contributions in this volume make a substantial and important contribution – not least because many are written not just by East European experts but also by representatives of the major countries of East–Central Europe who were themselves participants in the critical events of recent years. The contributions, while related in theme and subject matter, can nevertheless be divided into different groups. Amongst the first, Horváth and Szakolczai take a distinctive position on the limited impact of any East European civil society on the defeat of the communist state and direct attention to the self-defeating nature of the task undertaken by the communist regime and the methods used to carry it out. The must fruitful analogy to the operation of the party and its apparatus is to be found, they argue, in the activities of the police forces characteristic of absolutist states in the early modern period – a comparison which throws a searching light on the anachronistic nature of the Bolshevik project (particularly as transposed to the more advanced countries of Central Europe) and the lack of historical reality that characterised the rationality by which it operated.

They draw here a striking historical contrast which offers an original perspective on the increasingly-held conviction that the critical weakness of Soviet-style communism and the Stalinist path of development lay in its failure to secure the conditions for effective modernisation and construct the foundations on which a modern state could be be erected.[21] Related to this view were the cultural orientation and ideologies characteristic of the East European oppositions, prevalent in which were anti-political orientations and marked tendencies to reject the political values and practices of advanced, modern societies. Jørgensen, therefore, notes the ambiguities implicit in the idea of civil society and related concepts as applied to Eastern (and particularly Central) Europe and explores the complexities of the oppositions' ideological outlook. The idea of anti-politics itself emerges as a differentiated one which, further, required qualification and challenge from within the opposition before it could play its part in the developments that led to the transformations of 1989.

Nevertheless its traditions and influence linger on, retarding certain processes of political development and democratic change and continuing to pose questions about the future political nature of Eastern Europe. The amorphousness of social structure evident in communist Eastern Europe and the need to create, rather than extend or develop, a civil society is also emphasised by Tatur. She, however, pays particular attention to the consequences this had for gender relations and the failure of Eastern Europe to develop a women's movement. The conscious attempt to strengthen social structures and pursue strategies of social defence, most evident in Poland from the late 1970s, and one which followed the growing evidence of legitimation failure, tended to marginalise any questioning of sexual relations in the private sphere. Any moves in this direction were eclipsed by the production of 'society' as a political subject and the promotion of cultural traditions and the values of the immediate community as the basis for a reinvigorated social movement.

The struggle against communist dictatorship thus perpetuated an existing lack of differentiation between the private and social spheres which led, paradoxically, to a 'feminisation' of society and the strengthening of a general orientation to the domestic. This provided women with even less social space to pursue and secure their rights. The role of the Church, and particularly its centrality to developments in Poland during the 1980s, lent further force to this tendency. As Horváth and Szakolczai also recall, the nature of the party dictatorship in Eastern Europe reflected not just the role of the police in the absolutism of the early modern period but also that of the clergy as the other major obstacle in the struggle to establish the modern discourse of civil society. Civil society, in an older sense, was primarily understood to distinguish the sphere of civil or state power from the area of competence of church or religious power – and, indeed, Bobbio still maintains that 'religious society is neither political nor civil'.[22]

A further precondition for the development of civil society, one in fact closely associated with the role of the police and its powers of censorship, is the possibility of communicating in relatively unconstrained fashion throughout society – or at least with a significant proportion of its members. This, as Goban-Klas and Sasinska-Klas document, was an aspect of their power to which Lenin and (particularly) Stalin paid extremely close attention – but one where the leadership monopoly seriously began to break down very soon after Stalin's death. International and technological factors played an increasingly important role in this process, but so did domestic developments in terms of *samizdat* and the spontaneous growth of informal networks using primitive, if increasingly effective, technology which itself signalled some enhancement of social autonomy with respect to the power of the party–state complex. Even in a free society, though, communications systems and information technology require organisation and regulation, and thus they are inevitably involved in the broader political process. Extensive and relatively open communication may well be a prerequisite for an effective democracy, but the manner of its organisation and regulation can often provide a testing challenge for a new democracy.

Other contributions focus on the different stages of development (or, more precisely, decline) through which the communist systems have passed and contrast earlier approaches to the satisfaction of societal needs with those developing in the post-communist period. Morawski directs attention to the relationship between economic change and civil society in Poland. Early attempts at economic reform were restricted (replacing, essentially, direct forms of economic centralisation with indirect ones) and ineffective in the absence of a civil society and of social support for them. The situation prevailed for much of the communist period in Poland, up to 1980. Its evident failure gave rise to attempts at reform through socialisation, which grew out of moves towards social self-organisation in the 1970s and broadened into the initiatives made by the Solidarity movement. This approach, too, had little chance of success so long as the broader economic context and political framework remained unchanged.

It nevertheless persisted through much of the 1980s as Solidarity, the prime expression of the civil society that had developed, maintained the ideal of the new order as a 'post-state' and its established anti-politics stance. This, however, clearly began to break down in 1989 and the following period of intensified conflict within the Solidarity movement. Under these conditions civil society came to be seen not as successor to the state form (particularly, as had increasingly been recognised, in its socialist form) but as precursor of a developing democratic state. The evident shift to an economic emphasis in the social agenda for the 1990s nevertheless made this no easier a task to carry out in view of the contradictory assumptions and aspirations prevalent in Polish society. In another chapter, Wasilewski directs attention primarily to the political sphere and mechanisms of leadership recruitment, contrasting the procedures that dominated during successive stages of the communist period with the options open to the post-communist elite. In view of the high degree of popular sensitivity to earlier procedures and the role of the *nomenklatura*, decisions about future mechanisms and the fate of the existing bureaucratic apparatus are highly controversial and tend to be regarded as a touchstone of the democratic credentials of the post-communist elite. There are clear parallels between communist strategies and the solutions identified by post-communist elites, which in itself is not surprising, given the common nature of the problems faced by newly-installed ruling groups. Wasilewski outlines a set of requirements that should maximise the democratic character of the political transition process and emphasises the influence of the rapidly changing political context, which means that – so long as political life remains in flux and relations between the different political forces remain unstable – no final solution to the problems of leadership recruitment can be identified. The problematic nature of the transition and the solutions of the immediate post-communist phase emerges also in the chapter by Dölling.

Early hopes attached to the formation of a Women's Union in East Germany after the breaching of the Berlin Wall soon turned out to be largely illusory as, in association with the Green Party, the women's organisation gained a minute proportion of votes cast in the subsequent election. Post-communist developments, Dölling contends, have shown that the social support available for women under state socialism did not have an emancipatory character as they were directed to women in a functional sense – as workers or mothers rather than women in their own right. The subjective structures developed under the influence of these policies thus favoured the adoption of conservative solutions to the problems emerging in the process of transition. The roots of the problem lay in the dominance of the political over other orders within the communist system and the monopolistic form of representation practised by the party. This provided the basis for a form of patriarchal domination and the repression of tendencies towards the formation of a civil society which would permit the crystallisation and expression of particular social interests – including those of women (a conclusion similar to that reached by Tatur).

State socialism therefore perpetuated and reinforced, rather than counteracted, the male dominance of political life that was particularly evident in the nineteenth century and has left women with few resources to press their particular claims under the conditions' of insecurity that pertain during the period of post- communist transition. Even where elements of a civil society did develop more successfully, though, the prospects for the establishment of democratic procedures and the broader realisation of civil rights are by no means always good in the immediate post-communist period. Like Dölling, Mastnak surveys the situation after the transformations of 1989 (this time in Slovenia) and is by no means sanguine about the course of political developments. As he maintains, while civil society might be necessary for democracy to develop, it is not necessarily democratic in itself. Having experienced problems in controlling the activities of the new social movements, the state devolved some of its powers and discovered that civil society itself was better at exercising restraint over its more radical and unorthodox elements.

This form of social control, as a new exercise in direct democracy, he terms 'totalitarianism from below'. But it failed, too, and the new social movements that form the sinews of a modern civil society came to assert their strength and emerged as the focus for an unprecedented level of social mobilisation (now outlined by Mastnak under the heading of political society). Yet this also led to a reduction of social diversity as the independent sphere became more homogeneous and politicised, taking on a nationalist form to counter opposition from the multinational Yugoslav authorities (in which, however, Serbian influence predominated). The progressive democratisation of Slovenia (a process decisively shaped by the elections of the spring of 1990) meant, however, further transformation of the independent sphere and the marginalisation of its more unorthodox and radical elements – similar in some ways to the case of the East German women's movement outlined by Dölling.

The new form of democratically derived parliamentary power seems also, in this analysis, to imply new forms of dictatorial power – although this is ascribed not to a betrayal of the values of a civil society but to their realisation in a situation where the former restraints on civil society exercised by the communist state no longer apply. Finally Hann's argument is pitched at a less general level but it, too, is one that casts considerable doubt on the adequacy of any understanding of the pattern of East European developments that reduces its dynamics to the course and outcome of a contest between civil society and communist power. The communist order and the policies pursued within it, he argues, provided (at least in the Hungarian community with which he developed a close familiarity) conditions for the growth of a social cohesion whose survival is more likely to be threatened than assured by the forces gathering strength in the post-communist period.

The shock therapies and transformative strategies that have come to dominate the policy agenda of Eastern Europe may have considerably less positive implications for democratic development and the future of civil society than the gradualist pragmatism and policies of reformist socialism, seen mostly in Hungary, but whose influence was by no means absent from other areas of Eastern Europe. The lessons to be drawn from the experience of communism in Eastern Europe for the development of civil societies and the practice of democracy are, therefore, diverse and not reducible to simple formulae. One of the firmest conclusions that can be derived from that history is that simple solutions and policies reducible to a clutch of slogans are unlikely either to be successful or beneficial to the members of the societies to which they are directed. Similar implications may be drawn for the areas of social and political analysis. The spread of democracy and the growth of civil society have had lengthy and irregular careers, facts reflected in the controversies and intellectual debates which have surrounded them. The collapse of communism has served to open Eastern Europe further to these debates and challenges rather than drawn them to a conclusion.

Notes

1. R. A. Dahl, *Democracy and Its Critics* (New Haven: Yale University Press, 1989) p. 234.
2. S. P. Huntington, 'Democratization and security in Eastern Europe', in P. Volten (ed.), *Uncertain Fuitures: Eastern Europe and Democracy* (New York: Institute for East–West Security Studies, 1990) pp. 36–7.
3. P. G. Lewis, 'Democratization in Eastern Europe', *Coexistence*, Vol. 27, No. 2 (1990).
4. Dahl, *Democracy*, p. 263.
5. C. M. Hann, 'Second economy and civil society', *Journal of Communist Studies*, Vol. 6, No. 2 (1990) p. 31.
6. L. Schapiro, *Totalitarianism* (London: Macmillan, 1972) pp. 65, 69.
7. A. Stepan, 'State power and the strength of civil society in the southern cone of Latin America', in P. B. Evans, D. Rueschemeyer and T. Skocpol (eds), *Bringing the State Back In* (Cambridge University Press, 1985) pp. 318, 340.
8. J. Keane, *Democracy and Civil Society* (London: Verso, 1988) p. 22.
9. N. Bobbio, *Democracy and Dictatorship* (Cambridge: Polity Press, 1989) p. 22.

10. J. Frentzel-Zagorska, 'Civil society in Poland and Hungary', *Soviet Studies*, Vol. 42, No. 2 (1990) p. 759.
11. Z. Pelczynski, 'Solidarity and The Rebirth of Civil Society, in J. Keane (ed.), *Civil Society and the State* (London: Verso, 1988) p. 363.
12. J. Keane 'Despotism and democracy', in Keane, *Civil Society*, p. 36.
13. N. Bobbio, 'Gramsci and the concept of civil society', in Keane, *Civil Society*, p. 83.
14. J. Keane, *Democracy*, p. 14.
15. P. G. Lewis, 'Legitimation and political crises: East European developments in the post-Stalin period', in P. G. Lewis (ed.), *Eastern Europe: Political Crisis and Legitimation* (London: Croom Helm, 1984).
16. E. Shils, 'The virtue of civil society', *Government and Opposition*, Vol. 26, No. 1 (1991) p. 7.
17. Pelczynski, 'Solidarity', pp. 368-9.
18. A. Michnik, *Letters From Prison* (Berkeley: University of California Press, 1987) p. 145.
19. A. Arato, 'Civil society against the state: Poland 1980–81', *Telos*, 47 (1981) pp. 25, 27.
20. A. Melucci 'Social movements and the democratization of everyday life', in Keane, *Civil Society*, p. 250; 'Who's afraid of the toilet paper?', *East European Reporter*, Vol. 3, No. 2 (1988).
21. See Lewis, 'Democratization', pp. 252–4.
22. Bobbio, *Democracy*, p. 36; *The Future of Democracy* (Cambridge: Polity Press, 1987) p. 55.

1 The Discourse of Civil Society and the Self-elimination of the Party

Árpád Szakolczai and Ágnes Horváth

In explaining the revolutionary changes that occurred in Eastern Europe during 1989, one often encounters a discourse centring upon the resurrection of civil society. This seems all the more plausible as the concept of civil society was revived and used in East Central Europe extensively throughout the decade of the 1980s in a normative sense of promoting organisation and gathering support for the change of the system. Nothing seems to be more natural than to claim that, after all, events proved the correctness of the strategy: the resurrected civil society defeated the totalitarian system – to use another concept that became much in vogue in the last decade.

Nevertheless a more thorough glance at what was actually happening does not seem to support this 'natural' scenario. The struggle of the civil society against the state would imply a certain degree of confrontation, some mass organisation and mobilisation for positive goals. Nothing like that happened in these countries. Quite the contrary; one could perhaps say that the changes occurred at a point where any type of mobilisation was at its lowest ebb. This holds true as much for mobilisation for the system as against it. There was a popular involvement in 1956 in Hungary, in 1968 in Czechoslovakia, in 1980–1 in Poland. Not so in 1989. At this period both the system and the opposition suffered from the same fact – indifference, even apathy. The only thing which mobilised people can be described in negative terms – a desire for escape (East Germany), or a certain type of consumer mobilisation (Poland, Hungary) that can hardly be connected with the general, noble considerations underlying the resurrected discourse of 'civil society'. It has more to do with Hobbes than with Locke, Paine or Tocqueville.

Thus we can hardly explain the fall of the regimes as being the result of an increase in popular pressure. Rather the chain of events was started by some other factors that made the changes even more unprecedented and interesting from the perspective of social and political thought. It was perhaps the first case in which the holders of power simply gave up their position without the existence of organised, massive opposition to the regime. The idea of the disappearance of all power, the withering away of the state was a well-known tenet of utopian, Marxian and Bolshevik thought, and an explicit aim of the 1917 revolution. We all know what it led to in the past. But the way the events of 1989 occurred in many countries of the region showed that, after all, there was one type of state power that Bolsheviks were ready to abolish: and that was the power of the communist state party itself. An order that showed arguable the most systematic control over a population that ever existed simply eliminated itself. In our interpretation, this type of complete loss and internal dissolution can only happen if it is realised that the rationality of the system was dubious from the very start.

In this chapter we shall concentrate on two distinct factors that had a decisive impact on the way the regime maintained itself in the past, and that – so we argue – have also a key role in the way it dissolved itself: the power of the word and the power of the party apparatus. Concerning the first, we claim that, in analysing a system that laid such an emphasis on words and discourses, it is important that the concepts we use should be situated and used properly. Concerning the second, we shall rely upon our research carried out among the communist party apparatus in 1988 and 1989, research that was made possible in all different sorts of senses precisely by the events of the last few years. In our interviews and questionnaires, the aim was to reconstruct the programme and rationality embedded in the activities of the state party; we tried to assess the functionality of the project.[1]

One of the most significant findings of our study was the realisation that the apparatus had lost its voice, and was increasingly shaken in the very rationality of its government. This occurred in a system where for long decades the overwhelming importance of the public, official, especially written word coexisted with what many saw as the outright absurdity of the whole regime. Now secrecy was always one of the important instruments of power and no power tolerates statements that attack, contradict or mock it. But only statements that were considered to be threats to the existing order led to prosecution. The type of statements that were considered to be threats to the existing order, further, provide a good indication of the sensitivity of the system. In the party-states there was an incredible degree of attention attributed to all sorts of statements concerning the performance of the system. Most attention was devoted to the prevention of any utterances against the basic rationality of the system. There was a certain spell, a thick veil of ideology that had to cover everything, and the holders of power obviously thought that any statement falling outside this veil which received publicity would present a threat to the whole order. In this sense, magical powers were attributed to the word.

The question of truth and lies occupies a central place in the literature about totalitarianism.[2] However our point here is not just the unveiling of ideology and lies, but the reasons behind the power of the word and the prohibitions against certain of them; reasons that point beyond the realm of ideology. They are concerned with the fact that the whole discursive programme of the system was nonsensical. Not just because there was no question of the power of the working class – that is just ideology – but because the positive programme that lay beyond this ideology was also absurd, unreal, impossible; it was out of place and out of time. It does not represent the answer to a twentieth-century problem; it is not even meaningful in the context of the twentieth century. It is just the answer to an obsolete, by-passed, seventeenth-century problem. There were hardly any cases in human history where such a system of power did exist. This explains the inferiority complex that drove it to act in the way it did. It *had* to make itself real. It had to impress its reality on the population, using ever more terroristic methods until the point of exhaustion. It had to stage show trials with individuals confessing from the depth of their souls in order to supplement the reality of the external terror with the terror of the internal truth, while each new attempt at reality and truth only made things more unrealistic and less true. It could make itself real only by suppressing and betraying everything but its noble ideals – where all this obviously questioned the seriousness of these ideals themselves. Terror and repression were not the essence of this system.[3] Rather terror was made at once possible and necessary by the untimeliness and absurdity of the whole phenomenon of Bolshevism was truly unique.

Bolshevik-type state parties rediscovered the early modern police as the hidden essence of history and development and replicated it in the modern bureaucratic state and in the form of political police. The latter recalled the former, the early modern 'police', in the missionary zeal for the transformation of society, an instrument with a frightening potential for total control, but one that nevertheless incorporated a different rationality and thus could never be used properly. In this sense it is interesting to note that, since the 1970s there has been a widespread feeling that the use of modern information retrieval techniques could have a terrible impact in the Soviet Union. But this has never happened, simply because, in this way, the vital personal connection in the process of information collection would have been lost. There was just no way for the party to use computers effectively in its information collection process. The crucial goal in this process was mobilisation, and the use of modern information techniques would have been incompatible with this aim.

The early modern 'police' represented a technique of government connected to the contemporary art of government, the theory of *raison d'état*, and an apparatus created for the performance of tasks allotted according to this theory. Its activities and manners cannot but recall those of the Bolshevik state parties. The 'police' ensured the connection, the link, or, to use a contemporary expression, the 'communication' between individuals; its aim was to establish and maintain social life – society itself. Its target was the whole social body in all of its living and daily relations; it attempted to give a positive foundation to daily existence and to create an organic community.

This early modern 'police' was a reality that was almost immediately forgotten with the emergence of liberal societies and the modern police, partly owing to its identification as the 'precursor' of the latter. A liberal myth projected the modern police back to the period of 'absolutism', which was then identified as part of its reign. Still, as is increasingly realised in the West (starting from theoretical concerns that have nothing to do with Eastern Europe), an understanding of this obsolete meaning and reality of 'police' is particularly important as the revolutions around the year 1800 happened precisely against *this* police.[4]

The functions attributed to this early modern 'police' are surprisingly identical with those of the state party; even the words used are often the same. For example, there is a common concern for that which provides the 'ground' of political community. A particularly widespread metaphor concerned the 'columns' or the 'pillars' of society. Let us contrast here two seventeenth-century works, by Turquet and la Mothe.[5] Both mention four such 'pillars' and, in each case, these correspond to different branches of the (nascent) state. Three are identical; these are the army, justice and finance. The fourth is different; and in both cases it is the most important, as it provides the underlying foundation of the whole edifice; it is, if you like, the 'pillar of pillars'. For la Mothe, it is religion; for Turquet, it is the 'police' – perhaps the first case where the word 'police' is applied in a concrete, institutional sense meaning a technique of government and a body called to administer and execute these tasks. It is an important step in the long march from the Aristotelean concept of '*politeia*' to the modern police force, and, as we would argue, following a different path, towards the state party as well. Finally we should also mention that the concept of the 'pillar' is often associated in this literature with the bourgeoisie.

But perhaps the most important shared characteristic of the early modern 'police' and the Bolshevik-type state party is the preoccupation with order, the need to establish and maintain order at any price. One can refer both to the burgeoning theoretical discourses on the general question of order in the sixteenth and seventeenth centuries – why does order exist; what is the nature of order and so on – and to the correlative political literature on how political order can be maintained and assured. Given the civil and religious wars of the sixteenth century and the wars, espeically the Thirty Years War of the seventeenth century, this preoccupation was understandable; but even in the late seventeenth century it seemed that the predilection survived even when no longer functional.[6]

On the one hand, we have here a preoccupation with the basics of society, in an active, founding sense, both with the early modern 'police' and the contemporary state party; on the other, a concern with all sorts of activities and in minute detail. Our empirical study of the district-level party committees of Budapest demonstrated that, even in 1988, almost any economic or social activity was deemed worthy of the attention of the party, be it the development plan of the district council, the market price of cucumbers, the provision of schools with computers, or the sitting order in the common refectory of a school and a factory. And it is enough here to glance at the titles of the books of the enormous survey of the police by De La Mare – four volumes published, over three thousand pages, containing only the first six of the projected twelve books – to show that the early modern police had a similarly all-encompassing range of activities.

De La Mare's work is a compendium of regulations; and the German *Polizei-ordnungs* of the same period are also ordinances, regulations, papers. But there also came into being at the same time an apparatus whose task was the supervision of the execution of these resolutions, the relation between ordinances and apparatuses being exactly analogous to the relation between the party resolutions and the apparatus. Resolutions are quasi-legal regulations in the same way that ordinances were. The latter had the same binding effects as laws had, but they were passed solely by the king, without having recourse to the popular representative bodies. And the apparatus that was called to execute these resolutions was also highly specific.

It is almost an unquestioned commonplace to use the discourse of 'bureaucracy' in the description of the party apparatus. However, in spite of certain similarities, this is a mistake. We should make the same revision here as that done in recent works on the early modern period.[7] The discourse of the bureaucracy applied to the early modern period is anachronistic, especially for the description of the 'private service' of the king (as opposed to the civil service of the emerging state 'bureaucracies'. And the most important agents of the police – or similar apparatuses or institutions – were exactly related to the court, and to the king personally. They had a very particular relation to the traditional administrative organs and the population at large. They stood outside the whole formal legal framework. They were special envoys for specific, emergency purposes; for a long time, they had no fixed residence. The requirements of their jobs show that one cannot talk about bureaucracy in any sense of the term.

Let us take two examples here, comparing early modern techniques to the tasks of the political instructors. First the intendants of Colbert. In our study of the party apparatus, we assessed two major external tasks of apparatus members: the representation of the party, meaning at the same time the representation of the given line, the concrete resolutions and the more elusive sense of representing the 'Party' as a mythical–mystical entity, and the collection and dissemination of information. Here our analysis centred on the importance of personal elements, direct, face-to-face contacts as the condition for the performance of the multiple, manifest and hidden functions associated with the trade of information inside the state party. If one compares these findings to the analysis of the activities of the intendants by James E. King, the analogies are quite remarkable.[8] According to King, the tasks of the intendants can be described by the same two concepts, and even the methods of their accomplishment are almost identical. Colbert's instructions also used almost the same language, the same analogies and tricks that party instructors elaborated in 1988 and 1989: concerning the need to be informed about minute details, and not just broad overall trend; the need to establish friendships and to use these intimate connections for the collection of 'real' information, and so on.

The second example is even more surprising, as it comes from a country where the early modern police as an apparatus did not exist at all – England. But the court existed in the same way as in France (one should not forget that, for a long time, the Italian and the French courts represented the desirable model for the English court) and the kings did use special enoys – the members of the Privy Chamber.[9] The quasi-mystical manner in which these envoys represented the king had much in common with the way the party was 'represented' by the political instructors with some obvious differences: thus the belief in the mystical powers of the king was shared by the whole population in the sixteenth century, while in twentieth-century Eastern Europe such belief was restricted to party members (or, at least, they were supposed to believe in this mystical substance). The question as to whether in reality it was met or not belongs to the curious games of the 'voluntary compulsion' played in these countries,[10] towards the understanding of which this chapter would like to make a contribution.

Besides the type and scope of the activities and the concrete tasks of the apparatus, there are numerous analogies between the early modern police and the state party concerning the manner of their implementation, the languages used and so on. There is the well-known statement that, without the party, there would be complete chaos and anarchy; its equivalent with respect to 'police' can be found in the work of Turquet.[11] There is the recurrent idea, in the textbooks of that boring pseudo-science, the political economy of socialism, of the 'harmonic and proportional' growth of the socialist economy, the exact analogy of which can be found in a number of early modern works.[12] Or, to give a very concrete example, there is the prohibition concerning the industrial activities of agricultural enterprises that was in effect in Hungary up to the end of the 1970s, the elimination of which was considered to be one of the proofs of the benevolence and the smartness of the system of 'late paternalism'; a restriction that has no meaning whatsoever in the twentieth century, but that can be found word for word in the classic work of *Polizei-wissenschaft*, Justi's *Elements of Police*.[13] This work is a beauty in itself, the closest model of the socialist textbooks on political economy. If we take away from the latter the ideological garbage concerning the working class and the progress of socialism, we may recover all the major positive tenets in Justi's book. This amazing similarity can perhaps explain, not what Marx meant by placing Hegel the right way up, but what Marx's version of Hegel actually amounted to, as the grounds of Hegel's views on civil society were laid down by the activities contained in and related to the *Polizei-wissenschaft* of Justi. Hegel's famous metaphor about the owl of Minerva gives a very graphic account of how this recapitulation happened. In this sense, the Bolsheviks were only too faithful to the original Marxian scenario.

The same analogy can be observed concerning the way police administrators should carry out their job. Modern civil servants must be efficient, responsive and responsible, but they do not have to exhibit particular zeal towards their job. Quite the contrary; this would be dysfunctional, as it would disturb the ordinary daily business. Not so in the case of Bolshevik *apparatchiks* and early modern police officers. Early police treatises are full of enthusiastic claims about serving the public good. According to Duchesne, they should throw themselves with enthusiasm into all sorts of social relations;[14] and even the well-known Italian economist, Verri, exclaims at the beginning of his treatise about how much he would like to make some useful contribution to the public good.[15]

The zeal which police officers – and party functionaries – were supposed to exhibit not surprisingly led to comparable attitudes being expected on the part of the population at large. First they had to inculcate in the population the belief that, no matter what problems they have, they can always turn to the police. According to De La Mare, police officers should disseminate in the population the opinion that, if anything happens to anybody, he or she should immediately feel that the police is there to help.[16] This means that police officers must be constantly available. In our study of the role of the communist party in Hungarian villages, we found the same concerns and met with exactly the same sentences. We heard that the door of a village party secretary must be open day and night; that he or she should take personal care of any conceivable problem of the inhabitants, from the provision of bread to the acquirement of foreign medication; that he or she must be the first up and the last to go to sleep in a village. This latter statement, incidentally, has a long history – it was first applied to the Roman censors: an institution that was deemed particularly desirable at that early modern period in general. And this leads us to our second point: officers who take such minute and loving care of the fate of their subjects demand full respect from them. This is a respect which censors did gain in the past – such famous figures as Cicero or Cato started their careers as censors; and in eighteenth-century France, a high-level police job also meant good prospects for a future political career. Now while for modern police officers this career and the desired public admiration is obviously out of the question, both eighteenth-century police officers and Bolshevik party secretaries asked for the same respect; and to some extent, they did receive from some people something comparable. As for the rest, they relied upon something censors did not need and eighteenth-century police administrators could not have – the terror of the modern political police. The ideal–typical function of Roman censors is in itself very interesting, both in the early modern and in the Bolshevik context, as it represents a curious combination of moral and repressive functions.

Finally we may mention the self-importance and exuberance of French and Prussian police administrators, their use of contemporary science for purposes of social engineering, and their belief in their own importance and mission, comparable to the arrogance and – in a sense limited in time and space – innocence of their Bolshevik counterparts. It is not easy to reconstruct the reasons behind such activities, as the exercise of power is always hidden behind a thick layer of justification. Nevertheless the specific rationality of power can be excavated through an analysis of the discursive components of the activity, as the concrete ways in which power is exercised possess a certain particularity. In the case of the 'police', there is one motive that always comes to the fore, and that is the direct, overriding importance of the promotion of the public good. In modern societies, the idea of the public good also lies behind all sorts of public service, state administration, the activities of professionals and experts, and the functioning of the economic system as such, both as programme and as ideology. But the contribution of all these services to the common good is indirect, ultimate and not immediate; and, most important, it is not connected to a single apparatus or institution. Something comparable to the early modern police would be completely devoid of all meaning in a modern framework.

In the early modern period this was obviously not the case, as a large amount of intellectual effort was spent in defining the scope and reason for the activity of the police, and in administering these tasks. And not only was the task of directly serving the public good meaningful, but it was connected to an overall project of forming and transforming all sorts of social relations; it was connected to the transformation of the whole society, or rather the creation of a society as such. As was increasingly realised, again and again, by a number of different writers, 'absolutism' was not just a vehicle for the despotism of the king, not just the pursuit of cameralist policies in the interest of an army, nor mercantilist policies to help and support monopolies; it was a comprehensive project, endowed with its own sense of mission. One could say that *mutatis mutandis*, especially discarding the ideological baggage related to the working class, Bolshevism set out on a very similar project of social engineering, with a very similar sense of mission. Most importantly, this gives Bolshevism its specificity, setting it apart from earlier Asian despotism, or contemporary Latin-American or South-European authoritarianism, centred on the domination and exploitation of the subjects. In this sense, there are only two precedents for Bolshevism – the emergence of the modern state, with its theory of *raison d'état* and its police; and Christianity, with its similar mission to transform reality. This does not make the reality of Bolshevism more acceptable; quite the contrary; it becomes more insupportable. The most totalitarian aspects of this system result precisely from its missionary attempts at a positive transformation of society, from this specific civilisatory zeal. At this point it is worth remembering that, besides the police, the other major enemy of the modern discourse of civil society, liberalism and enlightenment was the clergy.

While thus we may risk the suggestion that Bolshevism meant a repetition of the programme of the secular transformation of society first attempted by the early modern states, the reality that surrounded it and that was produced was obviously far from identical in the two cases. Living in the France of Louis XIV, the Prussian of Frederick the Great, or the England of Henry VIII was an experience quite incomparable to the experience of living in Bolshevik Russia. Perhaps that is the reason why such historical comparisons were never much in vogue, although time and again there appeared works that drew attention to the significant similarities between 'bolshevism' and 'absolutism'. It is only as a result of recent revisions in the concept of absolutism and of methodological excursions concerning the epistemological status of the history of thought that a serious analysis of the similarities between early modern Europe and the Eastern European party states has become possible. It is an analysis that does not require the identity of lived daily reality to be established in order to make an assessment of structural, or rather programmatic similarities.

The Bolshevik state parties, thus, are not the same things as the police of the early modern period. They belong to a different stage in history, and to a different geographical region. But the programme, the rationality that is embedded in and can be excavated from the regular, daily activity of the apparatus of the state party is the same.

This historical excursion may help to explain why it is that the discourse of civil society is revived today in Eastern Central Europe in its classical, early nineteenth-century form; as one element in the revival of the classic liberal programme. The basic problem lies, not with the revival of an innocent, outdated liberalism in Central Eastern Europe, but in the deployment of an early modern institution in the twentieth century. In spite of a number of structural similarities in the 1940s between Central–Eastern Europe and early modern Western Europe, the problems were not the same. Although old methods of social and political control did survive, they became contaminated with modern elements. The experience of centuries of the civilising mission of the state, the traditional police state, was seen in Hungary, Czecho-slovakia and Poland. The way the new elements were accommodated in the old framework was perhaps not qualitatively but only quantitatively different from the situation in Western Europe, where it had been a fact of life – and also a matter of conscious policy – that novelties were always wrapped up in old clothes. But the Bolshevik attempt to redeploy these outdated methods was unnecessary and doomed from the start. Something was blatantly out of place. A certain type of discourse, a technology of power, were used that were the answer to a different problem; perhaps that is why it was not possible to use the indirect method, employed in the seventeenth century, of leaving the old framework intact. While this system was so repressive, it was also absurd and grotesque; it operated as if something was not in the proper place; it deployed a sophisticated machinery without tolerating any dissent, only to realise later that the problem was not the one for which this machinery was developed – as if it were the mistake of the patient to have the wrong illness, not the one to which the cure was applied.

Still two factors made possible the deployment of this system, the construction of a material reality out of a discursive absurdity. The first was the destructive impact of the world war – the first in Russia, the second in East Central Europe – creating a situation resembling that which saw the original emergence of the police, the period of religious and civil wars, and then the Thirty Years War; and second, the fact that Eastern or Central Eastern societies were not sufficiently modernised.

Concerning the first: modern society was created through a series of investments in certain mechanisms of discipline and control, that can by no means be described as an 'organic development' – another example of the current innocent myths in Central–Eastern Europe – or as *the* necessary path of civilisation. Rather one can observe a highly specific, definite series, whose starting-point is provided by a bloody war, always bloodier than anything that has previously existed, the key elements of this series being the Hundred Years' War; the Italian wars, starting with the invasion of 1494; the civil and religious wars of the sixteenth century; the Thirty Years War; the French Revolution and the Napoleonic wars; finally the two world wars. These were wars that led to increasingly great mobilisation and destruction; that provided legitimacy and popular support for the actions of the centre before, during and after the wars; where the methods used in the wars and by the army provided models for civil administration; and where, finally, the pressure of waves of social engineering was followed by move-ments to emancipate the social and the individual, but where this social and individual was – had to be – built on the debris of the previous, wartime and peacetime destruction and forcible reconstruction.

The model that proposes the separation of the state and the civil society thus seems to provide an insufficient account of the depth of these transformations, where the major problem is that the 'enemy', or what is perceived as such, cannot be reduced to an external body, but is situated inside the social body itself. On the other hand, it does not mean the inexorable victory of an always growing and extending state; that depends on our ability to resist and assert ways of life that are irreducible to the principle of governmentality.[17] There is now a period in Eastern Europe when the question of which direction will be taken is posed. It seems to us that an adherence to an early nineteenth-century liberal discourse with full zeal and complete innocence represents, not just the rejection of an alternative, but the very lack of realisation that such an alternative existed at all. And if this is the case, then the alternative perhaps does not exist – it has no materiality, no possibility. The absurdity of the Bolshevik discourse will be carried one step further.

Concerning the second factor, the insufficiency of previous modernisation efforts has made it possible to attempt the 'full' realisation of the potential of modernity and progress. This project, aiming at the complete mobilisation of society for the realisation of the common good, did have an immediate appeal both for part of the masses and for some members of the elite. But as soon became obvious, the concrete project resulted in a step backward being taken, rather than a step forward. The modern state represented the depersonalisation of government, while the party personalised it, made it the court of the ruler. It represented an absurd reversal of the Western European process, where personal envoys in the early modern period represented an important strategy used by the princes to establish and complement the modern state apparatus.

The same absurdity happened with another crucial target, mobilisation. The goal of the early modern state was to mobilise the whole population for the productive and military goals of the state. This was not particularly successful. The new discourse of liberalism and the civil society around the turn of the nineteenth century claimed to represent and mobilise the whole society against the earlier mobilisation attempts, which had been interventionist and oppressive. The result was a new compromise, not a clear victory for any of the protagonists. But perhaps the most lasting and important aspect of all this was related to the new levels of mobilisation. We have reached 'an important stage here in a long process, where the despotism of power leads to ever new and intensive, more complete mobilisation of the whole society, the whole personality; with more and more demands for the willing, complete and devoted adherence of individuals; where the personal will is dissolved in the political, in the quest for a perfect society, without power. The results are, and will be, new compromises. This creates two problems. On the one hand, the complexity of these new compromises will always prepare the terrain for the redeployment of the liberal critique of government (in a neo-liberal or other form), which means questioning and annihilating some of the hard-won concessions. On the other hand, to use a chemical metaphor, the progressive dilution of personal and interpersonal relations will perhaps be the most lasting and irreversible result of all these changes, as the successive struggles require an ever-increasing devotion to the new causes, destroying the distance between the political and public and the personal and the intimate; and, as one consequence, redeploying the uniqueness of human experience, relations and energies into the circumscribed, limited, 'secured' locus of 'the private'.

While mobilisation in the name of the civil society is thus not an unmixed blessing, the end of the communist system was caused not by this mobilisation, but by complete demobilisation. One could perhaps say that, as long as it was possible to mobilise the population, the communists also effected a counter-mobilisation. Once all possibility for such mobilisation and counter-mobilisation was gone, the system ceased to be able to function. This may explain the fact that the fall of the system was accompanied by very little popular enthusiasm. In Hungary, in Poland and in Slovenia, people clearly expressed their wish to end the communist party's hold over the government. But, while a few decades ago it would have been – and was – met with enormous relief and popular enthusiasm, now the reception was markedly subdued. In our study of the political events and attitudes of one Hungarian county, it was clear that the recent changes happened against a background of complete demobilisation of social forces and apathy.

According to an English saying, each family has a skeleton in its cupboard. In the case of Bolshevism, there was nothing else in the house. Thus the skeleton is not just the bureaucratisation of the party; not the fact that the working class is not the true bearer of history, or that the party is not the party of the working class; not even the millions of victims of the terror, and the incredible details concerning the management of terror. It is the complete absurdity of the core of the whole project itself.   '

At first glance, the party gave an answer that seemed plausibly to confront a number of crucial concerns and troubles of the twentieth century in Eastern Europe; it did perceive certain problems and internal contradictions in the way elements of capitalism and liberalism were accommodated within the existing power hierarchies in the East; moreover, following Saint-Simon and Marx, it gave some view – from a highly peculiar perspective – of the internal problems of the liberal method of government. In this way it could pose as a more advanced, post-liberal method of government when, in reality, it only took over from Marx what was, even in Saint-Simon, the most obsolete part of the analysis: the resurrection of the old system of welfare 'police' that was originally deployed, one may say, with some simplification, in the name of the creation of a bourgeoisie, from the perspective of the proletariat. Again in a strange way, it resurrected mechanisms that were used in the seventeenth and eighteenth centuries for the purpose of the 'civilisation' or 'embourgeoisement' of those who were not yet civilised, for the proletarianisation of all social classes – while the project of 're-bourgeoisement' appeared as a radical counter-discourse to the official doctrine.

Notes

1. On 'programmes', see Michel Foucault, 'Questions of Method', in *I & C*, No. 8 (1980); and Colin Gordon, 'Afterword' to Michel Foucault, *Power/ Knowledge* (Brighton: Harvester Press, 1980). For an overview of our research, see Ágnes Horváth and Arpád Szakolczai, 'The Dual Power of the State-Party and Its Grounds', in *Social Research* (Summer 1990).
2. See, for example, the works of Havel and Solzhenitsyn that put a particular emphasis on the question of truthfulness.
3. This was the view of Hannah Arendt, in her *Origins of Totalitarianism*, 2nd. ed. (New York: Harcourt, 1958).
4. For revisions of 'absolutism', see, among others, the works of Philippe Ariès, Norbert Elias, Roger Mettam, Gerhardt Ostreich and David Parker. For a reappraisal of the role of the 'police', see Michel Foucault, 'Omnes et Singulatim: Towards a Criticism of "Political Reason", in S.M. McMurrin (ed.), *The Tanner Lectures on Human Values* (Salt Lake City: The University of Utah Press, 1981).
5. See Loys de Mayerne Turquet, *La monarchie aristodémocratique* (Paris, 1611); and François de la Mothe Le Vayer, *Oeuvres* (Paris, 1662).
6. See Peter Miller, 'On the Interrelations between Accounting and the State', in *Accounting, Organisation and Society*, 1990 and Nicolas De La Mare, *Traité de la Police*, Paris, 1705–38.

7. On the question of bureaucratisation and Tudor government, see the pioneering work of Geoffrey Elton. (For example, *The Tudor Revolution in Government* (Cambridge: Cambridge University Press, 1953).) It is at /this point that we would take issue with the remarkable attempt of John Keane to come to terms with the nature of communism from a Western socialist perspective, and to construct a critical discourse of power in both the East and the West, by comparing the resurrection of the concept of the civil society in Eastern and Western Europe. (See his *Democracy and Civil Society*, and the collection of essays edited by him, *Civil Society and the State* – both London: Verso, 1988.) In spite of certain similar aspects of bureaucratisation, the concept of bureaucracy misses the key characteristic of the power of the party that lies in more direct, person-to-person methods, related to the perceived need for mobilisation as opposed to the mere administration of the population. On the question that the party is not a bureaucratic organisation, see Abdurakhman Avtorkhanov, *The Communist Party Apparatus* (Chicago: Henry Regnery, 1966); Jerry F. Hough, *Soviet Prefects* (Cambridge, Mass.: Harvard University Press, 1969); Philip D. Stewart, *Political Power in the Soviet Union* (Indianapolis: Bobbs-Merrill, 1968); and Aryeh L. Unger, *The Totalitarian Party* (Cambridge: Cambridge University Press, 1974).
8. See James E. King, *Science and Rationalism in the Government of Louis XIV, 1661–1683* (New York: Octagon Books, 1972).
9. See David Starkey, ('Representation through Intimacy', in Ioan Lewis (ed.), *Symbols and Sentiments* (London: Academic Press, 1977).
10. For the concept of 'voluntary compulsion' see Unger, *Totalitarian Party*, p.31. On the 'mystical' attributes of party membership, see also Yuri Glazov, *To Be or Not to Be in the Party* (Dordrecht: Kluwer, 1988).
11. See Turquet, *Monarchie*, p.69.
12. See ibid., pp. 6, 16; and Antoine de Laval, *Desseins de professions nobles et publiques* (Paris, 1613) p.319.
13. See Johann Heinrich Gottlob von Justi, *Eléments généraux de police* (Paris, 1769) p. 86.
14. See Duchesne, *Code de la Police* (Paris, 1767) p.8.
15. Quoted in Joseph A. Schumpeter, *A History of Economic Analysis* (New York: Oxford University Press, 1954) p.178. At that time, economics was taught as a branch of the science of police, as can be seen also from the Glasgow lectures of Adam Smith.
16. In the words of De La Mare, whenever anything troublesome happens, 'the first thing that should come into one's mind and the first remedy to be used should be a recourse to a commissar of police'. Moreover this should involve not only floods, murders or accidents, but 'even the differences that arise in families among the closest persons, or between neighbours or people of the same occupation; these should be brought before them [i.e. the commissars] and they should be the first judges for instructions; and, most often, the pacifiers.' (See Nicolas De La Mare, *Traité de la Police*, Paris, 1705–38). In this sense, it is particularly intriguing that the country where this maxim was realised the most thoroughly is the United States (on the extremely wide range of welfare-type non-repressive daily police activity there, see James Q. Wilson,

Varieties of Police Behavior, Cambridge, Mass.: Harvard University Press, 1968); the country that is considered, since Hegel and Say, to be the home of civil society.

17. On governmentality and its relation to civil society, see Michel Foucault, 'Governmentality', in *I & C* (1980) No.8; and the papers by Colin Gordon and Peter Miller in Graham Burchell, Colin Gordon and Peter Miller (eds.), *The Foucault Effect: Studies in Government Rationality* (Brighton: Harvester Press, 1991).

2 The End of Anti-politics in Central Europe

Knud Erik Jørgensen

Introduction

Before the year of revolution 1989, oppositions in Central Europe were, in Soviet and East European studies, by and large, regarded as marginal phenomena.[1] Certainly the emergence of Solidarity was a challenge to this priority, but no change in perspective seems to have occurred. Studies of politics in the region were reduced to studies of institutional politics and oppositions were consequently excluded or reduced. The 1989 systemic changes in the region should have changed this perception. The new governments in Central Europe are all based on previous opposition movements: Solidarity in Poland, Obcanské Forum in Czechoslovakia and Democratic Forum in Hungary. Thus important questions include the relation between continuity and change in Central European political culture and, more specifically, relations between the political culture of the oppositions and contemporary Central European politics. In this perspective, studies of the oppositions are not made obsolete as new political systems are introduced. On the contrary, such studies can be regarded as a precondition for the understanding of contemporary politics in Central Europe. If this view is accepted, the next question may be: do we know the political culture of the oppositions? To answer this question, a short digression into a subdepartment of Soviet and East European studies might be useful.

During the 1970s only a few studies on East European opposition emerged,[2] and in the early 1980s it was recognised, probably as a result of events in Poland 1980–1, that the phenomenon of opposition in Eastern Europe had been 'quite neglected' in Soviet and East European studies.[3] It does not seem unjust to repeat this conclusion a decade later. It is, however, not my allegation that such studies have been totally absent. It was not only Linden's conclusion that was induced by the Polish revolution. It also provoked a general interest in East European oppositions, which materialised in several studies. Priority was, not surprisingly, given to the Polish opposition,[4] but East European oppositions in general were also analysed.[5] Implicit in some studies was a theoretical and conceptual innovation which prompted consideration of new concepts like social movements and civil society.

Despite this growth in the number of volumes and a fruitful conceptual development, it is my proposition that research in oppositions has remained outside mainstream Soviet and East European studies. Thus, to Lovenduski and Woodall,[6] the study of East European dissent could be justified for analytical and ethical reasons. Analytical aspects were emphasised as 'dissent may disrupt the regimes and its potential must therefore be assessed in any overview of East European politics'. However this was not a perspective that saturated an otherwise openminded approach. Consequently, existing knowledge is limited and the political culture is generally unknown. This is even more true if we regard the political thinking of the opposition.

This chapter is in three sections. It begins with a discussion of a theoretical model combining social movements and development of political theory and ideology. The model is inspired by a Marxian–Gramscian theory of ideology and contains an implicit critique of Mannheimian relativism and the elitism of Pareto and political science in general. In the second section the model will be applied in a tentative discussion of the political theory of the Central European opposition. The vastness of the subject and its complexity, however, mean that it is mainly the important category of anti-politics that is discussed. The category itself is highly ambiguous and five dimensions are identified and discussed. The final section considers the process of political differentiation and ideological crystallisation evolving from the late 1980s. Although *raison d'état* considerations are bound to change some views and belief systems, it is the thesis of this chapter that the realm of oppositional political ideas, political outlook and fundamental belief systems is largely unchanged or closely related to former positions.

THEORY AND KEY CONCEPTS

Oppositions and the role of dissent have been studied as universal phenomena. However dissent has mainly been analysed in the context of Soviet-type societies. One reason to concentrate on Central Europe is that innovation in political culture has been more intense in this region (and in Germany) compared to France and Britain.[8] The comparative dimension in Hughes's approach will not be followed, but the assertion concerning political culture in Central Europe indicates a challenging perspective.

Political theory is a contested term, and ideology an even fluffier concept. It the predominance of anti-politics and ideological under-determination in Central European political culture is considered,[9] the introductory sentence needs to be further strengthened. The appropriate approach seems to be realism, vigilance and an open mind. I here try to come to terms with key concepts in political–ideological analysis, first by outlining perceptions of the opposition phenomenon; second, by discussing three approaches to the concept of ideology.[10]

Smolar argues that none of the proposed concepts is perfect.[11] He considers that application of the concept 'opposition', known from such different types of political systems as parliamentary democracy and traditional dictatorships, is tricky.[12] The competing term 'dissent' connotes, according to Smolar, a marginal phenomenon, individualism and derivation from the 'official Church', which, at least in the case of Poland, is an inadequate description. Smolar concludes, 'All these ambiguities of definition notwithstanding, I will use the term "opposition" simply because no other adequate word exists.' Thus opposition concerns the level of societal organisation. The view is related to Tocqueville's observations of societal atomisation as a precondition for state control. But it is not the only aspect in which Tocqueville seems to be a relevant point of departure. In line with a Tocquevillian tripartition between the state, political society and civil society, it has been argued that oppositions are also divided between the 'strictly political' and the broader cultural and economic activities.[13] To Smolar, a two-level pyramid can metaphorically represent an opposition. At the upper level one finds 'strictly political attitudes and activities aimed against the existing order'. At the lower level one finds 'all social, cultural, religious, educational and economic activities undertaken consciously to snatch fragments of public life out of the communist party's control'. Hence an inevitable ambiguity exists and a competing concept like civil society also implies problems. As remarked by Maier,[14] civil society and the public sphere are both topographical concepts. The classic study of the public sphere is Jürgen Habermas, *Strukturwandel der Öffenlichkeit. Untersuchungen einer Kategorie der bürgerlichen Gesellschaft* (1963). The category has been applied to Central Europe in several studies.[15] The approach of this chapter, that is to identify the sources of political thinking and subsequently to analyse the thinking, induces me to follow Smolar's terminology – with the provisos discussed by Smolar (and Havel). Thus oppositions are perceived as being engaged in conflicts and collective action and political thinking as originating in oppositions. It should be added that oppositions only in relation to the party state should be termed *the* opposition. As in civil society, a variety of opinions, groupings and ideological currents existed in the opposition.

In my discussion of theories of ideology, the point of departure is perceptions of ideology in two schools of sociology. In the classic tradition of Pareto and Mannheim ideology was defined by two functions and a concept of social elites. The ruling elite is using ideology as a source of legitimacy, whereas counter-elites count on the mobilising and integrative functions of ideology. For the third social force, the population, ideology was reduced to needs and excuses for basic psychological predispositions.[16] According to this perception, not unknown in modern sociology either, the ideology of the party state, Marxism–Leninism, nationalism and elements of welfare-state ideology have been used as a source of legitimacy. The counter-elite has, on the contrary, been using liberal thought, nationalism and elements of welfare-state ideology as means of mobilisation and integration.[17] Aspects of the elite versus counter-elite view were certainly present in György Konrad and Ivan Szelenyi's *Intellectuals on the Road to Class Power* (1979) and if one follows the logic, the Polish and Hungarian 'round tables' of 1989 were nothing but negotiations between competing elites. In studies of political theory and ideology it is, consequently, only necessary to study elites.

An opposite position is represented by Alain Touraine.[18] He emphasises the importance of activists in social movements. Touraine argues that participants in social movements are not simply a layer led by immediate interests transformed to political programmes and strategies by leaders of the movement. Touraine's approach implies the development of a new method, termed 'method of sociological intervention', but also that political–ideological documents and 'ideological language' in general are viewed as unimportant. The arguments are similar to a trend in social history, which also emphasises the social and downgrades the political–ideological dimension.[19]

Thus a dilemma seems to exist between the elite and the activists. But is it necessary to accept the dilemma? Are dialectical relations between theory and ideology, between elite and movement excluded *a priori*? According to a third model, dialectical relations are possible and they are perceived as a key to explaining development of political theory and movements.[20] The model is a synthesis of Marx, Weber, Gramsci and Heberle. The key elements are two assumptions and three comprehensive concepts. First, it is assumed that social movements are, historically, a rather modern phenomenon, that is, they came into existence after the French Revolution; second, that some kind of relationship exists between social movements and political theory/ ideology. The three concepts are 'social movement', 'ideology' and 'theory'. There follows a short outline of the three concepts.

Social movements are, in the classic study by Rudolf Heberle,[21] perceived as different from interest groups, political parties and protest movements. The reason is that they aim 'to bring about fundamental changes in the social order, especially in the basic institutions of property and labor relationships'.[22] This perception is not unique. Touraine[23] and Habermas[24] have emphasised a similar understanding of new social movements – in contrast to the main trend in literature on new social movements. To Heberle, the term 'movement' connotes 'a commotion, a stirring among the people, an unrest, a collective attempt to reach a visualized goal, especially a change in certain social institutions'.[25] This indicates that the level of organisation can be high, but this is not necessarily so. A sense of group identity and solidarity, however, is required: 'only when acting individuals have become aware of the fact that they have sentiments and goals in common – when they think of themselves as being united with each other in action through these sentiments and for these goals – do we acknowledge the existence of a social movement'.[26] And finally: 'A genuine social movement, on the other hand, is always integrated by a set of constitutive ideas, or an ideology, although bonds of other nature may not be absent'.[27]

How does this apply to Central Europe? One of the difficulties in applying a theory like Heberle's to the oppositions in Central Europe arises because the oppositions in a historical structural perspective can be located at the crux between old and new social movements. It is possible to identify features of both kind of movements. Heberle's analysis was developed for studies of classic social movements, but new social movements require a different approach.[28] Thus, in the Solidarity movement, several dimensions coexisted.[29] Second, mono-graphical studies, like Sørensen's, of *the* social movement as a working-class movement only, are not appropriate in the case of Central European oppositions, which have been a multifarious phenomenon. The diversity existing in the approach by Heberle seems more appro-priate. Third, it is, in the case of Poland, difficult to overlook the emergence of social movements in the early 1980s.[30] But did social movements exist in the late 1970s, or in Czechoslovakia and Hungary? The answers have generally been negative and oppositions have con-sequently been perceived as a marginal phenomenon.[31] According to a different perception, Vaclav Havel's (the Czech) opposition is 'one of the manifestations of the independent life of society...the most visible, at first sight the most political and ... the most clearly articulate... although not necessarily the most mature or the most important'.[32] This perception, in short, of the 'tip of the iceberg', could possibly also be applied to Hungary. Mass demonstrations in Czechoslovakia in the autumn of 1989 and the elections in 1990 proved that the opposition evoked a significant response in the populations. The different perceptions may be explained by reference to the approach chosen. If political studies are confined to institutional politics, then oppositions of the Central European type are excluded *a priori*.

If we turn to the concept of ideology, the point of departure is three quite different schools: mainstream political science, the sociological Pareto–Mannheim tradition and a particular tradition within Marxism (Lenin, Lukács and Althusser). In the three schools, ideology is typically characterised by negative connotations, as something distorted, false, reified or simply illusions. Political theory and philosophy are, in contrast, characterised as scientific, true knowledge or studies without value-judgements.[33]

In the Gramscian theory of ideology a complex relationship is established between theory, ideology and philosophy.[34] In the Gramscian-inspired approach ideology is perceived as similar to the three schools mentioned above, but it is *complemented* by a different concept of ideology that could be termed 'mass theory' or 'Ideology II'. It is defined as belief systems and attitudes to the social and political sphere, generalisations, based on everyday life, about social and political phenomena and prescriptions of action.[35] The important feature is that ideology can be not only false and distorted facts, but also true cognition at a mass level and usually within social movements.

When analysing ideologies in Central Europe the definitions discussed above might be insufficient. A supplementary distinction between ideology and mentality has been proposed by Juan Linz[36] and applied by Jadwiga Staniszkis in her *Poland's Self-Limiting Revolution*. In Linz's terminology, ideology is 'more or less intellectually elaborated and organized, often in written form, by intellectuals or pseudointellectuals or with their assistance'. Linz's definition of mentality, inspired by the German sociologist, Theodor Geiger, includes 'way of thinking and feeling, more emotional than rational, that provides noncodified ways of reacting to different situations'.[37] Typically mentality includes symbols and political myths.[38] The distinction between mentality and mass theory/ideology may be useful analytically, but in reality the concepts seem to be more or less synonymous. If so, it is not ideological under determination, but overdetermination that has been characterising the region. And precisely the immanent, subjective nature of ideology has caused problems when political solutions have been outlined.

Theory is defined as more articulated and systematic developed generalisations about the social and political sphere.[39] It is viewed as an attempt to reach authentic cognition beyond ideological distorted facts. Thus close and tensional relations exist between ideology and theory. In Gramsci's terminology, political theory is developed by 'organic intellectuals'. If this view is applied, part of the oppositions have functioned as 'organic intellectuals', albeit Central European-style. Finally 'declared ideology' is defined as 'movement ideology'; that is, party programmes, congress resolutions, speeches by leaders and activists. Journals and newspapers issued by movements are also considered declared ideology.[40]

It is in the realm of theory and declared ideology that I will, in a tentative way, locate the intellectual opposition. And I think it is in the same sphere that the intellectuals in the democratic oppositions have seen themselves. A few examples might be necessary to illuminate the claim. First, according to Michnik in 'the new evolutionism', 'the democratic opposition must be constantly and incessantly visible in public life, must create political facts by organizing mass actions, must formulate alternative programmes ... and defend basic principles'.[41] Second, Havel is expressing the same view in his 'The Power of the Powerless'. In this perception Solidarity's programme and the *samizdat* press as well have been part of declared ideology. The development of political theory through internal discussion took place in such journals as *Beszelö, Krytyka, Samorządność*. Thus it is a huge task to present a comprehensive analysis of the political theory and ideology of the Central European oppositions. In this sketchy analysis an attempt is made only to highlight the perceptions of a few key concepts.

THE POLITICAL THEORY OF THE OPPOSITION

Characterisation of political thinking involves several difficulties. References to ideologies and ideologues have been, with few exceptions, absent in oppositional political thinking. The phenomenon has been termed 'ideological underdetermination' and is apparently a late echo of Daniel Bell's thesis of 'the end of ideology'.[42]

However key concepts used in political discourse, such as 'civil society, solidarity and public sphere, are well-known from social philosophy and the history of political thought and this certainly complicates the picture. How do we relate conceptualisations of Central European experiences and traditional political thought? It is a tricky business and every kind of ideological short circuit is possible. In the following, three approaches will be discussed.

First, Zielonka traces, in his dissection of Solidarity's social thought, elements of French syndicalism, utopian socialism and anti-state collectivism,[43] syndicalism, with its 'emphasis on the revolutionary trade union, both as an organ of struggle (the general strike being its most potent tactic) and also as a foundation on which the future free society might be constructed'.[44] However he also notes the lack of historical inspiration and explains that in KOR 'contradictions and discussions were evoked by questions of tactics and method of action rather than by basic ideological problems. This context of discussion causes KOR to recognize doctrinal ancestry neither in the work of Kropotkin or Bakunin, nor in the work of e.g. J.S. Mill, H. Spencer, L. Bernstein or R. Luxemburg'.[45] However the absence of direct references could be explained by immanent ways of thinking. Hence the level of analysis ought not to be ideologies as systems of thought but type of action, concepts and perceptions.

Second, in his search for New Right political tendencies in Central Europe, Scruton takes any reference to Burke and Hans Kelsen, any apolitical position and any statement positive to market economy as a sign of New Right political thinking.[46] This approach is, to say the least, risky. The point of critique is not that syndicalism and New Right tendencies are non-existent. They certainly do exist and the existence of ideological currents gives new perspectives to the analysis of Central Europe. But the approach seems reductionist and non-dynamic. Contextual principles, so necessary in analysis of Central European politics, are not applied. In his discussion of autonomous politics, Goldfarb makes the same critique of theoretical inadequacy (in studies by Singer, Staniszkis and Touraine).[47] His excessive solidarism, however, results in another kind of biased approach. He favours Hannah Arendt as a guide to post-totalitarian politics. This is very understandable. Her 'tendency to substitute a poetic of politics for systematic analysis'[48] may be a problem, but her emphasis on freedom as constituted by politics and her sensitive understanding of the pre-political as a precondition for politics is highly relevant. Sometimes one gets the feeling, when reading Havel, that he is paraphrasing Arendt.

A different approach, almost etymological, has been chosen by

Ash,[49] Rupnik[50] and Smolar,[51] not to mention Havel.[52] In the following discussion of key concepts this approach will be used as a model. In continuation of the theories on social movements and ideology, outlined in the previous section I will focus on the essays by oppositional intellectuals as contributions to debates within the opposition concerning the system (party state) and its features; and concerning the opposition: identity, method of action, 'what ought to be done' and generalisations of experiences. Relations between theory and collective action are viewed as important, hence also questions of strategy and tactics. Finally the general blurring of the political, the social and the cultural has important methodological implications.

One consequence of the changed status of the political in Central Europe implies that we ought to look beyond the political essays of Havel, Michnik and the Hungarian János Kis. If literature functioned as the second parliament, then not only Havel's *The Anatomy of a Reticence* is relevant, but also his play *Pokuoseni*; not only Michnik's *Letters from Prison*, but also Tadeusz Konwicki's novel *A Minor Apocalypse*. In fact, in many essays the literary and the political interact. Although I cam convinced that this inclusion is essential in a profound analysis, I will not, for pragmatic reasons, include literary texts as a source of political thinking, in this chapter.

A key characteristic of the political theory of the opposition has been so-called 'anti-politics', which is usually not defined as a specific, concise term. This causes serious problems, also in the context of Central Europe. My starting-point, however, lies in Western Europe. When analysing new social movements Offe mentioned anti-politics along with competing concepts such as new politics, neo-romanticism, new populism and disorderly politics. In Offe's analysis, anti-politics was borrowed from Suzanne Berger's 'Politics and Anti-politics in Western Europe in the Seventies' (1979), but it was used simply to pin down the phenomenon Offe was analysing. He preferred the term 'non-institutional politics' to designate the thinking and action of new social movements being neither private nor public in the traditional sense.

In her analysis Berger argued that two trends of anti-politics emerged in Western Europe. First, the *nouveaux philosophes* in France, who had the non-communist New Left as direct ancestors, developed an anti-political position. The anti-politics of May was reformulated in the new philosophy 'in a full-scale assault on political power. It is not simply socialism that leads to the concentration camp, in the view of the new philosophers; it is all of modern thought from the Enlightenment ... all political conceptions of the world are oppressive and the only moral

stance is to resist the powers-that-be and the powers-that-would-be.'
The second trend and, in the view of Berger, more significant, is the
response by the new wave of non-institutional politics to the 'state's
deadening weight in individual and social life'.[53]

If we go back to the analysis of politics in Central Europe, it has been
claimed that anti-politics was one of the common positions in the
writings of Havel, Michnik and Konrad.[54] It is, however, doubtful that
'anti-politics' can be characterised by the one-dimensionality claimed
by Ash. First, because, in the category of anti-politics, perceptions of
system and opposition were combined; second, because the concept
seems to be multidimensional. One method of handling this multi-
dimensionality is to define more precisely what is perceived as anti-
politics and what it not. In Hella Mandt's sophisticated analysis this
method is applied.

She is first arguing *ex negativo*, delimiting the term from meaning
simply a divorce from political activity and the adoption apolitical
attitudes. Anti-politics has nothing to do with 'shifting involvements'.
The term is further delimited from a specific German tradition reaching
from von Humboldt to Thomas Mann (*Betrachtungen eines Un-
politischen*, 1918) and others. Finally anti-politics is perceived as
different from 'Apolitie'; that is, a temporary retreat from the public.

The core of anti-politics has rather to do with a conscious and
fundamental contempt for or hostility towards politics as a specific type
of human activity; it originates from a multitude of contradictory
opinions and interests. Thus anti-politics transcends the elitist attitudes
of John Stuart Mill: 'In a settled state of things, the commanding
intellects will always prefer to govern mankind from the closets, by
means of literature and science, leaving the mechanical details of
government to mechanical minds'.[55] Anti-politics is in this way the
negation of Hannah Arendt's perception of politics as a Sisyphean
conditio humana. Mandt traces anti-politics back to an anarchist social
critique as represented by Proudhon and Bakunin. But she also traces it
back to different types of religious convictions, to German romanticism,
and to the 'classical' representative of anti-politics, Rousseau, who
inspired the young Marx as well as Carl Schmidt.[56] In the analysis of
the political theory of the Central European opposition, Mandt's
contribution is very useful. In the following, consequently, an attempt
will be made to relate Mandt's definition to the theoretical discourse of
the opposition. However, for analytical reasons, I would suggest a
discussion along five dimensions:

* 'anti-politics' as critique of power *per se*;
* 'anti-politics' as critique of state power;
* 'anti-politics' as critique of fusion;
* 'anti-politics' as a question of tactics;
* 'anti-politics' as critique of international bloc politics.

The most comprehensive critique is naturally of power *per se*. Havel's approach, partly based on Husserl's concept of the 'life-world' and Belohradsky's critique of 'politics as a rational technology of power', is partly a critique of power *per se*. But it is not a critique of politics as such, only of certain types of politics. Masaryk also seems to have influenced the thinking of Havel. Key concepts like truth, non-violence and 'non-political politics' characterised Masaryk,[57] as well as Havel. In fact Havel favours what he terms 'anti-political politics': 'that is, politics not as the technology of power and manipulation, of cybernetic rule over humans or as the art of the useful, but politics as one of the ways of seeking and achieving meaningful lives, of protecting them and serving them. I favour politics as practical morality, as service to the truth, as essentially human and humanly measured care for our fellow humans'.[58] Consequently Havel attempted constantly to downgrade the importance of the directly political in the traditional sense and to emphasise the importance of the pre-political terrain. The approach is simultaneously a critique of sections of Charter 77 (the reform communists, among others) which sought power or influence and those, such as Petr Uhl, who viewed Charter 77 as a revolutionary avant-garde.[59] Havel's position makes it difficult to argue that Havel thinks within a tradition of anti-politics as defined by Mandt. At the same time it is also important to recognise that Havel's involvement in politics is temporary: 'I will continue to devote myself to politics until normal professional politics are revived in this country. Then I will be able to go back to the Theatre on the Balustrade, perhaps as Karel Steigerwald's assistant repertory adviser'.[60] It seems more relevant to relate Konrad to anti-politics, which has been an important theme in several of Konrad's essays,[61] but even in this case it is difficult to argue that Konrad is a representative of fundamental anti-politics.

From another perspective it could be claimed that Konrad, and also Havel, verbalises a general mood in the Central European population. The attitude has been explained by Vajda: 'Deep down, however, there is always something much more simple, more palpable, more lifelike than any abstraction: "Let me be, leave me alone, don't try to tell me how to live".'[62] Vajda places this mentality in the context of paternalistic traditions in the region. He describes how these people, maybe with Czechoslovakia as an exception, are 'dreaming of the "good king", not of the mature responsibilities of democracy'.[63] A Romanian slogan from 1989 crisply expressed the attitude: 'We want democracy – we don't want politics.' It is quite obvious that both Havel and Konrad are conscious of this predominating mentality in Eastern Europe, but in the case of Havel this consciousness was also combined with a critique of power. It is a challenging perspective to perceive the opposition's critique of power as a continuation of traditional Central European perceptions of power and rationality – Max Weber and Norbert Elias (*Über den Prozess der Zivilisation*, 1939) being the most important.

Second, the critique of state power is part of a detotalising strategy in which civil society played the crucial role. From Michnik's 'new evolutionism' to Havel's 'living in truth'; from Benda's 'parallel politics' to Konrad this dimension of 'anti-politics' is a key element in political thinking. further the dimension is present not only in theories, but also in declared ideology of the Solidarity movement, that is, the programme from 1981, 'the self-governing republic'. The present economic programmes of deregulation in Central Europe are a direct continuation of these theories. It is surprising that Scruton does not use the concept in his eagerness to demonstrate the existence of a 'New Right'. He refers only to Michnik's reference to Burke's *Reflections on the Revolution in France* and to a general 'apolitical' attitude.[64] To Rupnik,[65] critique of state power also relates to the region's traditional *étatisme*; that is, to the 'endogenous factors which could have played a role in the establishment of Communist systems'. Thus Rupnik perceives the critique as a continuation of Hayek and von Mises' critique of modern *étatisme* based on its Austrian incarnation.

The critique of the disappearance of politics is based on a specific interpretation of politics, after which politics has disappeared in a general 'elimination of the autonomy of subsystems'.[66] According to Bihari, 'the result of the total politicization of the economic system and the economization of the political system was the fusion of these two subsystems and the total disappearance of their relative autonomy'.[67] Consequently, anti-politics is not a choice but a condition. Culture as a subsystem could be included as well in the total fusion, thereby explaining the 'culturisation of politics' so evident in Central Europe. However I will proceed by mentioning some consequences of the fusion.

Traditional categories such as Left and Right were regarded by Michnik and Havel as supremely irrelevant. In Michnik's words,'"To the vast majority of Poles "Right" and "Left" are abstract divisions from another epoch' and Havel says: 'I admit that it gives me a sense of emerging from the depth of the last century'.[68] The view is, however, more representative for Havel than for Michnik. For a long time Michnik was regarded, and regarded himself, as a leading representative of the left–liberal tradition in Poland. In *Kosciol, Lewica, dialog* (1977) he was a spokesman of the left. In KOR he belonged to the *Krytyka* 'faction' and he contributed to the establishment of the political club KSR-WSN in November 1981.[69] In the essay 'Conversation in the Citadel' (1982) he also discussed the socialist tradition in Poland. The paradox between Ash's anti-political Michnik and the self-identification can be explained in terms of flood and tide: 'At that time [the 1970s] the right did not like the label "right"; today, the left does not like its traditional identity. This contredanse has also been observed in places other than Poland.'[70] In Hungary, too, the concepts were fading in importance. As remarked by Judt, the real shock for Miklós Haraszti 'was not learning that the old categories of Left and Right were defunct, gone forever, but realizing that everyone already knew this'.[71] Whether the categories have gone forever will be discussed later. We are here looking for the substitutes offered.

If left and right categories were irrelevant, what was relevant? To explain this we have to enter the sphere of the pre-political. Havel and Michnik are offering moral categories: right–wrong, lie–truth, dignity, duty, sacrifice and so on. As Ash puts it, 'Moral categories figure largely in the writings of the three authors (though less in Konrad than in Havel and Michnik). All three reassert the fundamental premises of Judaeo-Christian individualism'.[72]

The application of pre-political categories corresponds to the existence of mentality rather than ideologies in Central Europe. In terms of ideology it is a period of interregnum. The dominant ideology was ritualised and the opposition was not able or ready to crystallise new ideologies. However mentality in Central Europe is a multifarious phenomenon. It contains *universal* elements, like pre-communist political traditions, mixed with mentalities rooted in Soviet-type societies. In contrast, symbols and political myths play a crucial role in *specific* national political cultures.

The fourth element of political theory to be discussed is strategy/tactics. The theoretical analysis of the oppositions contains at the same time the elements of a political strategy. The essays answer questions of tactics and strategy like Lenin's 'What is to be done?' and are often written in a specific context. They are committed to critique or dialogue between persons, groupings or movements. The discussion within the movements is one type of framework frequently debated.[73] They contain tentative answers to 'situations' or events. Before, during or after: if after, as attempts to generalise experiences. According to Goldfarb, 'Michnik writes primarily occasional pieces which answer immediate political questions through historical, literary and political investigations'.[74] A striking similarity exists between, for example, Rosa Luxemburg's *Massenstreik, Partei und Gewerkschaften* (1906) and Michnik's *Letters from Prison*. Both are attempts to generalise experiences: in the case of Luxemburg, the Russian Revolution of 1905; in the case of Michnik, the Polish self-limiting revolution of 1980–1.

The overall strategy has been surprisingly unchanged since the mid-1970s, when the new oppositions emerged. But any attempt to outline the main strategy involves serious difficulties. Catchwords like non-political, non-conspiracy, non-violence, non-utopian, non-party and no political alliances or programmes have been typical. Thus negations seem to be favoured in the self-identification of the opposition, naturally perceived by the opposition as non-opposition too. The preference of negations can be explained by reference to tactical considerations or to level of development. If one tries to define what the elements of strategy were, the list of catchwords includes legalism, confidence in the force of example (but non-persuasive), open (non-exclusive and non-sectarian) and ethnic-moral appeals. Hence the political discourse includes categories which are atypical in the West European political discourse.

Historically Michnik's seminal essay on the 'new evolutionism' was a critique of revisionist and neo-positivist perception and strategy. Simultaneously a new strategy was outlined and the essay is described as 'the turning-point when the opposition ceased addressing the party state and turned rather to society itself'.[75] If Michnik's 'new evolutionism' was a critique of revisionist strategy, then his *Church, left, dialogue* (1977) expressed a rapprochement between the lay Left and the Catholic Church in Poland.

Thus it is a general problem to interpret the balance between tactics and principles. Ash quotes Michnik as an example of 'theoretical and ethical underpinning' of an anti-political strategy.[76] 'We suspect that by using force to storm the Bastilles we shall unwittingly build new ones ... Solidarity does not aspire to take power in the state', but a few years later, in 1988, Michnik's conclusion concerning 'what we can do' had changed dramatically, resting on a new perception of Gorbachev and the Soviet 'new political thinking' in foreign policy. As formulated by the *International Herald Tribune* in July 1988, 'The Poles have got a new Hero – a Russian'. The logical step followed one year later, in July 1989, when Michnik proposed exactly 'to take power in the state', although self-limited power; that is, a government led by Solidarity. The example shows that many positions were tactical, but interpreted as principles. I do not argue that Michnik is without principles. On the contrary, he has very consistent principles, but they are mixed with a remarkable sense of tactics.[77]

The symbiosis between theoretical analysis and strategy was not confined to Poland. Havel's essay, 'The power of the powerless', was written in 1978 as a contribution to a dialogue between Charter 77 and KOR and it also spurred a debate within Charter 77.[78] His essay 'The Anatomy of a Reticence' (1985) was a response to Western European peace movements and intended for the Peace Congress in Amsterdam. The 'Essay on Bravery' by Ludvik Vakulik provoked a long debate within Charter 77, a debate which, according to Milan Simecka, showed 'the central fault in current Czech dissident thinking'.[79] In Hungary the 'social contract' concept developed by Kis, Köszeg and Solt was also an attempt to answer immediate political questions.[80] This is miles away from Konrad's almost anarchistic critique of traditional politics and power.

The relationship between power and opposition developed, however, in different ways in different countries and the pattern of development influenced the type of opposition and hence the political thinking. There was variety in level of activity, alliances and degree of development. In the case of Poland, the interaction between political theory and social collective action determined a special type of theory, being more *directly political* than in the case of Czechoslovakia where action was generally confined to *symbolic* action. In Hungary the opposition engaged itself in more direct political action, but the conditions were different from the Polish ones.[81]

Some elements of the general strategy seem not to have been contested. One example is the doctrine of 'non violence'. To Ash, both pragmatic and ethical reasons existed. The lessons from 1956 and onwards suggested that a strategy of violent revolt would turn out to be a blind alley. However the reasoning has been in terms of Christian ethics like 'vanquish evil through good' and 'the conviction of the value of sacrifice'.[82] It should be added that during the Polish 'self-limiting revolution' the strategy was operationalised into 'occupation strike' tactics in order not to provoke confrontations in the streets. In Michnik's reference to the 'Spanish model', that is a peaceful transition from totalitarianism/authoritarianism to democracy and pluralism, the same line of argument is followed. However the introduction of martial law provoked a discussion within underground Solidarity about the usefulness of continuing the strategy of the 'self-limiting revolution', if the 'war of position' should be followed by a 'war of movement'.[83] The fifth dimension of anti-politics concerned perceptions of European identity and international relations. The catchphrase has been Central Europe. The debate on Central Europe was opened by Milan Kundera in 1983 with his seminal essay, 'The Tragedy of Central Europe'. According to Kundera, kitsch is perceived as the real thing in Western Europe and the United States. Kundera consequently publicised a retrospective utopia, a tableau of Central European intellectual history. With the reception of the essay, 'Central Europe' was introduced into the opposition's political discourse. Generally, the reception was highly critical, but a degree of reality was also recognised. Ever since this ambiguity has been both the strength and the weakness of the concept. From the beginning it served multiple functions and the concept itself is multidimensional: geographical, cultural, political.[84] The Central European kitsch was accompanied by the idea of a process of de-Europeanisation. For Kundera, the turning-point was 1968, but the general view has been that 'de-Europeanisation' was synonymous with state-socialism *per se*.[85]

The political dimension includes primarily geopolitical considerations. As civil society functioned to conceptualise Utopia and a sphere of action and power domestically, Central Europe has functioned at the international level as a critique of Yalta logic. Important differences existed between the national approaches. The Polish opposition regarded Central Europe as only a minor issue, maybe because the opposition was more engaged in political and even economic issues than in social and cultural issues. According to Judt,[86] Central Europe was not a project for the Hungarian opposition either, but it functioned as a critical tool of enquiry. For the Czech opposition, the concept functioned as an ontological creation, 'a metaphor for the other Europe which they seek to re-create'.[87]

Basically the critique of Kundera's essay included four points. First, the fact that, in Kundera's Europe, 'Russia' was excluded. The view was criticised, not only by Russians such as Lev Kopelev and Josef Brodsky, but also by the Czech, Milan Simecka. In fact the discussion is nothing but a continuation of the classic question concerning Europe's eastern border and with it the question of Europe's identities. Second, the Germanies were excluded, not from Europe, but from

Central Europe. It was never seriously contemplated that the end of
Europe's division included a united Germany, and a dialogue between
the Central Europeans and German supporters of the concept 'Mitteleuropa' was hardly ever established.[88] One important example of
dialogue was Jiri Dienstbier's *A Strategy for Europe. Through Central
European Eyes* (1988).

Third, the debate should not obscure the fact that identities in
Czechoslovakia, Poland and Hungary primarily are national and ethnic.
According to Kusy,[89] an East European identity did not exist. Identities
are national and ethnic and Central European if regional. A reflection
of this view can easily be identified in the political discourse of the
oppositions. Although Michnik refers to Czechoslovakia 1968 as a
relevant experience, he refers primarily to Polish national tradition,
represented by Abramowski, Piłsudski and Dmowski; in Hungary it
was people like Eötvös, Oscar Jaszi and István Bibó; in Czechoslovakia, a strong connection exists between Jan Patocka, Edmund
Husserl, Masaryk and Havel. Thus the main features are national
diversity and contradictions. Finally, the debate on Central Europe had
an analogous existence at the official level. In Poland the reception was
highly critical. Central Europe was perceived as a myth and only a few
found the debate interesting.[90] In Hungary the reaction was more
positive. In 1984, a new perception of the responsibility of small nation-
states in global politics was expressed;[91] later there was an attempt to
transform the concept from 'unhistorical' and 'unrealistic' features
with a 'nostalgic tone' to a 'modern' and 'realistic' concept.[92] To
suggest that this proves an agenda management capability or a Kuron-
like injection, 'our independence into dependent state structures' situation may be a too far-reaching conclusion, but, as Hajdu's example
shows, the concept and debate was a challenge to official politics.

The concepts discussed above are by no means the only ones in the
political theory. Totalitarianism was one of the most important. Jacek
Kuroń once stated in an interview that, if the opposition could give
something to the world, it was a comprehensive understanding and
conceptualisation of totalitarianism. Perceptions in the oppositions
were, however, accounted for in an examplary essay,[93] and also
prompted the approach chosen by Goldfarb.[94] The opposition also
reintroduced a Kantian language of rights, which gained legitimacy
from the (Helsinki) CSCE process (based on the Conference on
Security and Cooperation in Europe).[95] Havel has analysed the ideology of the party state or rather the ritualisation of official ideology.[96] A
striking similarity exists between Havel's concept and Linz's analysis

of ideologies in authoritarian regime forms.[97] The disintegration of human identity is a dominant theme in Havel's thought and a key to explaining why he has been emphasising the pre-political. Ideological ancestors have been analysed: in Poland by Michnik,[98] whose essays on Dmowski and Piłsudski are among the best examples. Thus a whole range of concepts and theories was gradually developed by the oppositions. In the next section the political thought during and after the 1989 revolutions will be analysed in order to demonstrate continuity and the transformation of anti-politics in Central Europe.

POLITICAL DIFFERENTIATION AND CRYSTALLISATION

The 1989 revolutions marked a dramatic turning-point. This is the very essence of revolutions. But there had been other important turning-points before, which explains why the revolutions were not only radical changes, but also a continuation of former traditions. Thus important elements of the general strategy and of anti-politics had been challenged from within the oppositions and changed accordingly. The most important changes were expressed in a proliferation of political parties and programmes from 1987 to 1988. This was an attack on one of the key elements of anti-politics. It was a general trend, but the timing, form and consequences were different in the three Central European states.

In Poland, the Solidarity experiment was experienced differently from those in Czechoslovakia and Hungary. The political trends gradually crystallising after the forced dissolution of Solidarity can be divided into three main tendencies: Church and church-oriented opposition, the realists and political radicals.[99] The realists were characterised by their willingness to co-operate with the regime. The locus of co-operation and expectations towards manipulation by the regime prompted Smolar to make a subdivision: government-oriented opposition, new realists and new anti-politicians. The activities of the latter, not to be mistaken for anti-political strategy, were, in Tocquevillian terms, within civil society; that is, citizens' private, mostly economic, activities based on self-interest.[100] The political thinking of the trend was openly liberal and anti-leftist. In the spring of 1987, the new realists created the political club 'Dziekania', thus integrating five political groups into a 'para-political Church-oriented entity tolerated if not recognized by the state'.[101]

The third trend – the political radicals – took the opposite view from the anti-political, legitimist opposition, known from the 1970s and from Solidarity's first 16 legal months: 'it is the system's core that must be attacked first ... the liberation of the country and the introduction of a democratic system are the direct objectives'.[102] The radical view on strategy did not exclude the fact that both radical left (KOS, Fighting Solidarity) and radical right (KPN) currents could be identified within the trend. In a far-sighted conclusion, Smolar recommended that 'these groups should be closely watched, if only because of the uncertainty and unpredictability of history. It is in them that political elites are being formed, a new language and old concepts are adapted to new conditions'.[103] With regard to Hungary, it is generally accepted that there were two main political trends in the Hungarian opposition during the 1980s.[104] The labels that have been used to characterise the first is 'Central Europeans' (Enzensberger), 'Cosmopolitans' (Barfoed), 'Westerners' (Kende) and 'urban-bourgeois' (in Hungary). The second has been termed 'populists' and 'nationals'. The differences concern the cosmopolitans' emphasis on universal principles versus the nationals' concern for the 'fate of the nation'.

Some members of the cosmopolitan trend were previously revisionist, that is reform communists, and belonged to the 'Budapest School'. Thus, their political–intellectual development has been similar to Kuroń and Michnik's in Poland.[105] In the late 1970s, the best known representatives, Bence and Kis,[106] still worked within a Marxist tradition, but, inspired by the Polish KOR and Solidarity experiments, they departed from Marxism a few years later.[107] The sources of the new political thought were anti-totalitarianism, liberal democracy and the Hungarian democratic tradition, represented by Eötvös, Jaszi and Bibo.[108] The break with Marxism took place relatively late compared with Poland and Czechoslovakia. In 1988, two movements, and later parties, Fidesz and SZDSZ emerged from the 'cosmopolitan' trend.

The tradition of Hungarian populism can be traced back to the 1930s and 1940s. Three observations seem relevant. First, Hungarian populism is described as 'more a state of mind, than a political ideology ... a current devoid of a premeditated doctrine but which can exist thanks to a shared awareness kept alive by a prolific literary output'.[109] Using Linz's terminology, it is a mentality rather than an ideology. Second, Hungarian populism has been engaged in a number of alliances with the Hungarian Communist Party. Thus it was more or less integrated in scientific and cultural institutions. Third, in the late 1980s, the new movement, Democratic Forum, emerged from populism as the largest movement in Hungarian opposition. The nationals 'have the wind in their sails both because of current events (the conflict with Romania) and because society as a whole is better prepared to reason on these terms than on the basis of abstract concepts, have found an adequate expression of their political thought in the Democratic Forum: an open movement, without a too compromising programme that criticises the regime but doesn't attack it directly and speaks to public opinion chiefly through coded messages'.[110]

Developments in Czechoslovakia were different. Continuity was the catchword and no important political parties emerged; politicisation of anti-politics failed to come off. However it should not be overlooked that Charter 77's self-confidence was increasing. In 1985, Havel concluded his essay 'The Anatomy of Reticence' in an optimistic way: 'history is unpredictable, and we need to be prepared for a whole range of eventualities: recall, for instance, how the dissidents of the Polish Committee for Defence Workers (KOR) had to become practical politicians overnight'.[111] Two years later, in a review of Charter 77's first decade, he concluded that history is 'back and open'.[112] The review also functioned as a contribution to the debate in Charter 77, on whether to engage in direct political organisation or proceed along the previous lines.[113]

Against this background the diversity between Central European oppositions is clear. In Czechoslovakia there is mainly self-confidence and hope. In Poland and Hungary there are several parties and a relatively well-developed oppositional 'infrastructure'. No wonder that the development of party systems in Central Europe followed different paths. Although the revolutions of 1989 caused some metamorphosis of belief systems, the basic pattern of political currents remained largely the same. It was rather the relative strength of the currents that functioned as the unknown factor.

The revolutions have been interpreted in very different ways. In Ash the search for some kind of order or pattern results in a chaotic picture of political–ideological ideas.[114] In Habermas's perception, it was a 'rectifying revolution' characterised by 'the desire to connect up constitutionally with the inheritance of the bourgeois revolution'; that is, a return to constitutional democracy. For Habermas, a peculiar feature of the revolution was 'its total lack of ideas that are either innovative or oriented toward the future'.[115] These are two challenging perspectives for those regarding the post-communist society as a solution in itself. To Ash, it is rather chaos and to Habermas a return to a 150-year-old formula.

If we look at the level of party systems, that is between Habermas's generalisations and Ash's picture of complete chaos, it seems useful to make a distinction between the *historical parties*, the *liberal political groupings without political precedents*, the *'follower parties'* and the reorganised *collective ruling parties*,[116] but as in Western Europe the pattern of the new political system includes a multiplicity of interest groups, parties and new social movements.

Hungary did not have movements like Solidarity and the Czech Obcanské Forum (Charter 77). During the dissolution of traditional power structures and the synchronous development of embryonic party structures in the late 1980s a slow process of political/ideological crystallisation was initiated. The process of crystallisation produced essentially six parties represented in parliament out of more than 50 parties registered with the authorities. The overwhelming victory of the Hungarian Democratic Forum (MDF) has been explained with reference to the party's ability to master the balance between the past and the future most convincingly to the voters: 'it was the only party which promised the citizens to gradually make a Western-type democracy of a one-party state while preserving the national values of Hungary's history at the same time'.[117] Café Gerbeaud in Budapest, as a political issue, may be illustrative of the concern about national history.[118] The strong liberal current, represented by SZDSZ and Fidesz, is extraordinary in a comparative European perspective. In a Hungarian context it is the strongest representation ever, as the country has never had a strong liberal movement.[119] The new political structure thus includes two corners of the classic triangle of European political–ideological currents: 'We can say that we find two major political centres in the political structure. One of these is the social–liberal, the other is National–Christian. And if something is missing it is just a line of social-democrats'.[120]

In Poland the heritage of the great 1980–1 Solidarity movement has proved to be an obstacle to political differentiation. A decade's collective memory implies that differentiation will be extremely painful. The mergence of major political groupings such as the Centre Agreement (PC) and the Civic Movement – Democratic Action (ROAD) within a diminished Solidarity shows that the process is inevitable, probably provoked by close links between Solidarity and the government of Mazowiecki.

In Poland the congruity between values and behaviour is higher than the congruity between interest and behaviour. In a survey from May 1990 the traditional left–right dimension did not exist. As an alternative it was possible to identify two distinct political cultures: a liberal–

democratic–cosmopolitan, emphasising free markets, pluralism and 'European' thinking, and a populist–nationalist–authoritarian, emphasising state intervention, national values and inward-looking. In 'The two faces of Europe', Michnik describes a similar pattern, arguing that the greatest danger to democracy is no longer communism, but a 'combination of chauvinism, xenophobia, populism and authoritarianism'.[121]

The two types should be viewed as ideal types and a certain mix should be expected in reality. On the basis of the survey it is predicted that the type of parties in Poland will be campaign parties as contrasted to parties based on socioeconomic interests. The necessity to have strong executives in systems with campaign parties is still unsolved, although institutions 'above politics', for example in the form of a strong presidency, have been created.

In Czechoslovakia six political currents have been identified: reform communism, social democracy, liberalism, Christian democracy, conservatism and environmentalism.[122] The existence of the Czech and Slovak nations is likely to duplicate, not the political currents, but the number of parties and movements institutionalising the currents. The first free elections, however, caused a limited pluralisation and differentiation as the Obcanské Forum got an overwhelming majority, leaving only a minor part of the votes to other parties or movements.

The gradual political differentiation and ideological crystallisation has important consequences at the theoretical level. Returning to the phenomenon of anti-politics, the 1989 revolutions placed the former representatives of anti-politics in the governments. This was the litmus test to establish whether anti-politics was of the fundamental type as defined by Mandt, or some kind of temporary device, developed as a response to specific circumstances.

It has already been demonstrated how important elements of anti-politics were demolished with the creation of political parties in Poland and Hungary. But this was part of a general trend. Anti-politics as *leitmotif* was gradually vanishing in the late 1980s in these countries. The complexity of the notion, however, determined several options. From the 1989 revolutions, the oppositions were no longer restricted to acting within the 'parallel *polis*' (or alternative political system), but were occupying the *polis* itself. The fission of the economic–political–cultural totality into traditional subsystems, each characterised by a relative autonomy, resulted in new conditions.

Anti-politics as a critique of fusion became increasingly irrelevant. One consequence could have been a reintroduction of the categories of

Left and Right, yet the reintroduction was to a certain degree hindered by a different type of anti-politics. The category of national independence has previously in this century obscured the right–left dimension in the region, and it has been reintroduced to a totally unexpected degree. Contradictions between the dividing lines based on ethnicity and on liberal political pluralism hinder a return of the categories of Left and Right.

Anti-politics as critique of power has gradually been removed to the cultural sphere. According to intellectuals such as Konrad the distance and independence of anti-politics will be preserved also in relations with new democratic governments.[123] Havel is in a precarious situation. To what degree is it possible to make 'politics of man, not of the apparatus. Politics growing from the heart, not from a thesis' as he wrote in the essay 'Politics and Conscience'?[124] His inaugural New Year speech seems to indicate that it is possible, especially if more symbolic dimensions of politics are emphasised.[125]

Critique of state power has been maintained and maybe to a problematic degree. First, radical critique of state power contributes to a classic dilemma between diversity and unity: 'The central problem of democratic politics in modern society is to maintain the diversity within civil society while creating some measure of unity, or bindingness, of political authority: *E pluribus unum*. This problem is more easily solved in political systems whose underlying diversity remains one of *interests*; it becomes more difficult when *values* or cultural models must also be mediated'.[126] In Central European civil societies dividing lines are, however, primarily based on values and cultural models.[127] Second, radical modernisation and deregulation is not only a means to an efficient economy and administration, but also results in such social problems as unemployment and individual insecurity.

The bloc-transcending capabilities of the concept 'Central Europe' have gradually been changed from the military–political East–West dimension to the economic–political centre–periphery (EC–Eastern Europe) dimension. The response to de-Europeanisation has been the 'Back to Europe' slogan. In foreign policy doctrines the bloc-transcending pan-European security structures were first emphasised, but later it was the dissolution of the Warsaw Pact combined with some kind of association with NATO. Further the regional pentagonal initiative has been presented as a microcosm of a future pan-European co-operation. So far, however, it seems more to be a potential modernised 'Kakania', with a powerful Italian bias. Thus, as opposition theorists were turned into newspaper editors, ministers and a president, the belief systems have to a certain degree been transformed, as *raison d'état* considerations have functioned as an inescapable imperative. It is, however, also possible to identify a strong trend of continuity in belief systems.

Thus anti-politics has in a certain sense ended its existence as a key feature in Central European political theory. But it is not totally absent, either from the political discourse or from the attitudes in the population. The low participation, especially in the first local government elections, demonstrates a continued existence in the population of mistrust or even hatred of politics. In fact, if one considers the region's traditions of static orientation, centralisation and absolutism, which is generally accepted,[128] the growth of pluralism and parliamentarism after the 1989 revolutions has been surprising. The socioeconomic transformations, however, have not yet been fully implemented and it remains to be seen if 'Weimarisation' of Central Europe is avoidable.

Two main trends seem to exist in the political–ideological landscape of *fin-de-siècle* Central Europe. One trend is characterised by populist, introverted and xenophobic ideas, praised in national movements and parties. The opposite trend, liberal 'European' and pluralist, is located on a liberal–social axis. Yet socialist and social-democratic positions are weakly represented, leaving the scene to classic liberalist values and thought.

Notes

1. Throughout this chapter 'Central Europe' refers to Poland, Czechoslovakia and Hungary. East Central Europe might have been a more adequate term. See, for instance, M. Vajda, 'East-Central European perspectives', in John Keane (ed.), *Civil Society and the State: New European Perspectives* (London: Verso, 1988); H. P. Burmeister *et al.*, *Mitteleuropa. Traum oder Trauma* (Bremen: Temmen, 1988); and G. Schöpflin and N. Wood (eds), *In Search of Central Europe* (Cambridge: Polity Press, 1989).

2. See, for instance, L. Schapiro (ed.), *Political Opposition in One-Party States* (London: Macmillan, 1972); P. Raina (ed.), *Political Opposition in Poland 1954–1977* (London: Poets and Painters Press, 1978); and R. Tökés (ed.), *Opposition in Eastern Europe* (London: Macmillan, 1979).

3. R. H. Linden, 'East European studies: groups, gegs, and gaps', *Studies in Comparative Communism*, Vol. 15, No. 4 (1982) p. 335.

4. See, for instance, J. Staniszkis, *Pologne – la révolution autolimitée*

(Paris: PUF, 1982); Alain Touraine, *Solidarité. Analyse d'un mouvement social: Pologne 1980–81* (Paris: Fayard, 1981); P. Raina (ed.), *Independent Social Movements in Poland* (London: LSE, 1981); A. Arato, 'Civil society vs. the state', *Telos*, No. 47 (1981) pp. 23-47; Arato, 'Empire vs. civil society', *Telos*, No. 50 (1982) pp. 19–48; and K. E. Jørgensen, *Den polske opposition – en analyse af den polske oppositions politiske og ideologistke hovedstromninger* (Aarhus, 1984).

5.   F. Claudin, *L'opposition dans les pays du 'socialisme réel'. Union Soviétique, Hongrie, Tchecoslovaquie, Pologne 1953–1980* (Paris: PUF, 1982); W. D. Connor, 'Varieties of East European dissent', *Studies in Comparative Communism*, Vol. 15, No. 4 (1982); J. L. Curry (ed.), *Dissent in Eastern Europe* (New York: Praeger, 1983); and T. Judt, 'The dilemmas of dissidence: the politics of opposition in East-Central Europe', *Eastern European Politics and Societies*, Vol. 2, No. 2 (spring 1988) pp. 185–240.

6.   J. Lovenduski and J. Woodall, *Politics and Society in Eastern Europe* (London: Macmillan, 1987) p. 340.

7.   See H. S. Hughes, *Sophisticated Rebels: The political culture of European dissent 1968–1987* (Cambridge Mass.: Harvard University Press, 1988).

8.   Ibid., p. 3.

9.   See Staniszkis, *Pologne*.

10. The model was developed by C. Sørensen, *Marxismen og den sociale orden* (Grena: GMT, 1976) and *Demokrati-diktatur problematikken i den centraleuropoeske socialisme politiske teori ca. 1925–35* (Aarhus, 1981).

11. A. Smolar, 'The Polish opposition', in A. Smolar and P. Kende (eds), *The Role of Opposition: The role of opposition groups on the eve of democratization in Poland and Hungary (1987–1989).* (Cologne, 1989) Research Project on Crisis in Soviet-Type Systems, pp.7–8.

12. Judt, 'Dilemmas of dissidence', pp. 186–7.

13. Smolar, 'Polish opposition', pp. 7–8; T. G. Ash, 'Der Niedergang des Sowjetischen Imperiums', *Lettre Internationale*, Heft 3 (1988) p. 22.

14. C. Meier (ed.), *The Changing Boundaries of the Political* (Cambridge: Cambridge University Press, 1989) p. 11.

15. Arato, 'Civil society' and 'Empire'; M. Molnar, *La démocratie se lève en Europe de l'Est* (Paris: PUF, 1990).

16. Sørensen, *Demokrati-diktatur problematikken*, pp. 42–2.

17. Lovenduski and Woodall, *Politics and Society*, pp. 421–32.

18. Touraine, *Solidarité*; Touraine, *The Voice and the Eye* (Cambridge: Cambridge University Press, 1980).

19. Sørensen, *Demokrati-diktatur problematikken*, pp. 64–8.

20. See Sørensen, *Marxismen*; Sørensen, *Demokrati-diktatur problematikken*.

21. R. Heberle, *Social Movements. An Introduction to Political Sociology* (New York:, Appleton-Century-Crofts 1951).

22. Ibid., p. 6.

23. Touraine, *The Voice and the Eye*.

24. J. Habermas, 'New social movements', *Telos*, No. 49 (1981) pp. 33–7.

25. Heberle, *Social Movements*, p. 6.

26. Ibid., p. 7.
27. Ibid., p. 11.
28. C. Offe, 'Challenging the boundaries of institutional politics', in Maier, *Changing Boundaries*; Touraine, *The Voice and the Eye*.
29. Touraine, *Solidarité*; Jørgensen, *Den polske opposition*.
30. Raina, *Independent Social Movements*.
31. Lovenduski and Woodall, *Politics and Society*.
32. Quoted in H. G. Skilling, 'Independent currents in Czechoslovakia', *Problems of Communism*, January–February 1985, pp. 81–2.
33. See Sørensen, *Demokrati-diktatur problematikken*, pp. 35–44.
34. The Gramscian connection has to be emphasised, as Gramsci is usually perceived as one of the most important *political* thinkers within the Marxist tradition. See P. Anderson, *Considerations on Western Marxism* (London: NLB, 1977); Sørensen, *Demokrati-diktatur problematikken*). In studies of Central European politics the connection to Gramsci is also recognised (see, for instance, Z. Pelczynski, 'Solidarity and the rebirth of civil society', in Keane, (ed.), *Civil Society and the State*) but a comprehensive application of Gramsci's political theory has not, to my knowledge, yet been attempted.
35. Sørensen, *Demokrati-diktatur problematikken*, p. 47.
36. In F. Greenstein and N. Polsby (eds), *Handbook of Political Science*, Vol. 3 (Reading Mass: Addison-Wesley, 1975).
37. Ibid., pp. 266–7.
38. Cf. K. C. Farmer, *Ukrainian Nationalism in the Post-Stalin Era* (The Hague:, Franks, CES., 1980).
39. Sørensen, *Demokrati-diktatur problematikken*, p. 51.
40. Ibid., pp. 53–4.
41. A. Michnik, *Letters from Prison and Other Essays* (Berkeley: University of California Press, 1987) p. 147.
42. Staniszkis, *Pologne*, coined the phrase 'ideological under determination'.
43. J. Zielonka, 'Social philosophy and the Polish experiment', *De sociologische Gids*, March–April 1983, pp. 82–93.
44. Ibid., p. 84.
45. Ibid., p. 88.
46. R. Scruton, 'The New Right in Central Europe', 2 parts, *Political Studies*, Vol. 36 (1988) pp. 449–62 and 638–52.
47. G. Goldfarb, *Beyond Glasnost. The Post-Totalitarian Mind* (Chicago and London: University of Chicago Press, 1989) pp. 119–57.
48. Ibid., p. 129.
49. T. G. Ash, 'Does Central Europe exist?', *New York Review of Books*, 9 October 1986, pp. 45–52.
50. J. Rupnik, 'Dissent in Poland 1968–78', in Tökés (ed.), *Opposition in Eastern Europe*.
51. Smolar, 'The Polish opposition'.
52. V. Havel (ed.), *The Power of the Powerless* (London: Hutchinson, 1985); Havel, *Living in Truth* (London: Faber, 1986).
53. S. Berger, 'Politics and anti-politics in Western Europe in the seventies', *Daedalus*, Vol. 10, No. 2 (1979) pp. 27–50.

54. Ash, 'Does Central Europe exist?'
55. Quoted in H. Mandt, 'Antipolitik', *Zeitschrift für Politik*, Jg. 4 (1987) pp. 385–6.
56. Ibid., pp. 386–90.
57. See J. Trojan, 'Democracy and its spiritual foundations', *East European Reporter*, Vol. 4, No. 3 (1990); J. C. Nyiri, *Am Rande Europas. Studien zur österreichisch-ungarischen Philosophie-geschichte* (Vienna: Böhlau, 1988).
58. Havel, 'Anti-political politics', in Keane (ed.), *Civil Society and the State*.
59. See P. Uhl, 'The alternative community as revolutionary avant-garde', in Havel (ed.), *Power of the Powerless*.
60. V. Havel, 'The arena I do not wish to enter', *East European Reporter*, Vol. 4, No. 3 (1990) pp. 38–9.
61. G. Konrad, *Antipolitik. Mitteleuropäische Meditationen* (Frankfurt: Suhrkamp, 1985); Konrad, *Stimmungsbericht* (Frankfurt: Suhrkamp, 1987).
62. Vajda, 'East-Central European perspectives', pp. 349–50.
63. Ibid., p. 348.
64. Scruton, 'New Right', p. 461.
65. J. Rupnik, 'Totalitarianism revisited', in Keane (ed.), *Civil Society and the State*, pp. 282–3.
66. Ibid., p. 282.
67. Quoted in ibid., p. 282.
68. Quoted in Ash, 'Does Central Europe exist?'
69. Jørgensen, *Den polske opposition*, pp. 159–63.
70. Smolar, 'The Polish opposition', p. 32.
71. Judt, 'Dilemmas of dissidence', p. 189.
72. Ash, 'Does Central Europe exist?'
73. See W. Machenbach, *Das KOR und der 'polnische Sommer'* (Hamburg: Junius, 1982); J. J. Lipski, *KOR, A History of the Workers' Defense Committee in Poland, 1976–1981* (Berkeley: University of California Press, 1985); G. Dalos, *Archipelag Gulasch. Die Entstehung der demokratischen Opposition in Ungarn* (Bremen: Temmen, 1986).
74. Goldfarb, *Beyond Glasnost*, p. 223.
75. Rupnik, 'Totalitarianism revisited', p. 284.
76. Ash, 'Does Central Europe exist?'
77. Judt, 'Dilemmas of dissidence', p. 227.
78. Havel (ed.), *Power of the Powerless*.
79. Judt, 'Dilemmas of dissidence', p. 226.
80. See E. Hankiss, 'Europe lost – and gradually regained?', *Südosteuropa*, Vol. 37, No. 10 (1988) pp. 574–98; Scruton, 'New Right', pp. 649–50.
81. Judt, 'Dilemmas of dissidence', pp. 197–8; Claudin, *L'opposition*.
82. Ash, 'Does Central Europe exist?'
83. Jørgensen, *Den polske opposition*, pp. 169–70.
84. B. Swiderski, 'Østeuropaernes Europa', in Hans Boll-Johansen and Michael Harbsmeier (eds), *Europas opdagelse. Historian om en ide* (Copenhagen: Christian Ejlers, 1988); C. Magris, 'Mitteleuropa – Realität und Mythos', *Lettre Internationale*, Heft 4 (1989) pp. 17–20; E. Jahn, 'Østeuropa og Mellemeuropa', in Jens-Jørgen Jensen (ed.), *Europa i opbrud* (Esbjerg, 1988).

85. Vajda, 'East-Central European perspectives', pp. 333–60; Hankiss, 'Europe lost?', p. 582.
86. Judt, 'Dilemmas of dissidence', p. 224.
87. Ibid., p. 225.
88. Ash, 'Does Central Europe exist?'
89. M. Kusy, 'We, Central-European East Europeans', in Schöpflin and Wood (eds), *In Search of Central Europe*.
90. See Swiderski, 'Østeuropeaernes Europa', p. 153.
91. See J. Rupnik, 'Eastern Europe and the New Cold War', in R. Crockett and S. Smith (eds), *The Cold War: Past and Present* (London: Unwin Hyman, 1987).
92. See A. Hajdu, 'On a novel approach to the concept of Central Europe', *Külpolitika*, English-language supplement (Budapest, 1988).
93. Rupnik, 'Totalitarianism revisited'.
94. Goldfarb, *Beyond Glasnost*.
95. Judt, 'Dilemmas of dissidence', pp. 191–5.
96. Havel (ed.), *The Power of the Powerless*.
97. Ibid., and Linz in Greenstein and Polsby (eds), *Handbook*, Vol. 3.
98. Michnik, *Letters*, pp. 201–22, 275–333.
99. Smolar, 'The Polish opposition', pp. 20–33.
100. Ibid., pp. 29–30; Pelczynski, 'Solidarity', p. 379.
101. Smolar, 'The Polish opposition', p. 28.
102. Ibid., p. 30.
103. Ibid., p. 33.
104. N. Barfoed, *Hotel Donau* (Copenhagen, 1988); P. Kende, 'Functions and prospects of the democratic opposition in Hungary', in Smolar and Kende (eds), *The Role of Opposition*, pp. 63–7.
105. Dalos, *Archipel Gulasch*.
106. G. Bence and J. Kis, *Towards an East European Marxism* (London: Allison and Busby, 1978).
107. G. Bence and J. Kis, 'On being a Marxist', *The Socialist Register* (London, 1980) pp. 263–97.
108. See Kende, 'Functions and prospects', pp. 63–4.
109. Ibid., pp. 64–6.
110. Ibid., p. 75
111. Havel, *Living in Truth*, p. 195.
112. *Information*, 17–18 January 1987.
113. Judt, 'Dilemmas of dissidence', p. 197.
114. T. G. Ash, 'Eastern Europe: après le déluge, nous', *New York Review of Books*, 16 August 1990, pp. 51–7.
115. J. Habermas, 'What does socialism mean today? The rectifying revolution and the need for new thinking on the left', *New Left Review*, No. 183 (September–October 1990).
116. M. Fülöp and L. Póti, *An East European Party Census*, Policy Paper Series No. 2 (Budapest: Hungarian Institute of International Affairs, 1990) p. 7.
117. F. Gazdag, 'The Landscape in Hungary after the Elections in 1990 (mimeo, 1990) p. 22.
118. *Frankfurter Allgemeine Zeitung*, 9 April 1990.

119. Cf. Z. L. Nagy, *The Liberal Opposition in Hungary 1919–1945* (Budapest: Akadémiai Kaidó, 1983).
120. Gazdag, *Landscape*, p. 24.
121. A. Michnik, 'The two faces of Europe', *New York Review of Books*, 19 July 1990, p. 7.
122. J. Pehe, 'The political spectrum', *Radio Free Europe Research* (1990).
123. Konrad, *Antipolitik*, pp. 213–14.
124. Havel, *Living in Truth*, p. 157.
125. These questions have also been discussed in a clear-sighted editorial, 'Still living in truth', *East European Reporter*, Vol. 4, No. 3 (autumn–winter 1990).
126. Offe, 'Challenging the boundaries of institutional politics'.
127. Ash, 'Eastern Europe'.
128. Hankiss, 'Europe lost?', pp. 578–82; I. Volgyes, 'Parliamentarianism and pluralism in East Europe', *East European Quarterly*, No. 3 (1987) pp. 265–74; A. Polonsky, *The Little Dictators. The History of Eastern Europe since 1918* (London: Routledge, 1975).

3 Why is There No Women's Movement in Eastern Europe?

Melanie Tatur

INTRODUCTION

The 'Women's Question' did not succeed in establishing a place for itself in Poland during the 1980s, neither within the framework of the social sciences, relatively free as they were from a political straitjacket, nor within the social movements and political groupings that existed. Until well into the 1970s, against the background of an expanding employment system, a whole branch of research investigated women's qualifications, career patterns, the forms and conditions of women's employment, as well as changes in the division of labour within the household and the structure of the nuclear family, but such research retreated completely into the background from the beginning of the 1980s onwards. The family and its socialisation function became the focus of interest instead. The question of sexual relations within the family and within society generally was relegated unproblematically to a position of secondary importance after the reproduction of society and the transmission of cultural traditions.

One exception was a report that appeared in the mid-1980s on the position of Polish women. It was perhaps characteristic that the initiative for this study originated from women working in the field of health research.[1] It does not inquire into the relevance of women's emancipation, but examines instead the level at which the physical health of women was threatened and the various dimensions of this threat.

One must search in vain for any relevant beginnings of a women's movement in the reactivating and organising society of the 1970s, of the 1980/1 period or the 1980s. The official 'League of Polish Women', for whom the emancipation of women was a central tenet, in the economic sense at least, and who had assisted in this respect in legitimising the removal of laws and regulations protecting women, was a discredited body.

New feminist initiatives in Poland are currently nowhere to be seen.

On the contrary: conservative social demands are being raised, such as the return of women to the family, the re-establishment of the sanctified nature of the family, and a ban on abortion, demands which are articulated by religious movements within and on the fringes of the Catholic Church. In milder form, such demands do indeed find a high degree of resonance, particularly among younger women from the educated middle strata; that is, among groups who in the West would typically be supporters of the women's movement.[2]

This is by no means a peculiarity of Poland. The situation is similar in the societies within the Soviet Union which are currently crystallising into a new shape. Within the nationalist movement in Estonia there is a women's organisation; its professed aim, however, is greater respect for the family, greater numbers of children, and the demand that 'our men' perform their compulsory military service in their own country and not within the Soviet forces.

One could try to find an explanation for the contrasting attitudes and aspirations of women in East and West in terms of the social situations of women and the historical background in each case. For Poland this would mean taking into consideration secure employment and the existence of careers for women in the feminised areas of the social services sector. Women are disadvantaged here, too, however, with respect to leadership positions, promotion opportunities and, above all, pay. In addition, being in employment does not as a rule guarantee a woman material independence on account of the generally low pay levels.

But it must also be mentioned at this juncture that women are held in high esteem in Poland, something that has its origins in Polish tradition, and which is still made visible today in customs and rituals. Furthermore there has been a rapid detraditionalisation of patriarchal family structures; the partnership dimension within marriage has come to the fore as a consequence of women receiving training and taking employment, not to mention the emancipation, indeed the virtual ennobling, of women's sexuality. These changes are characterised by a certain ambivalence – here, too, the division of labour within the household and in the family occurs at the expense of the woman and at the cost of her career aspirations, and it is also women who bear the brunt of the costs of sexual liberation, for example in the form of alarmingly high rates of abortion.

It could also be pointed out that there are differing perceptions of women's emancipation – in Eastern Europe as something ordered and forced on people 'from above' while in the West women advanced into the labour market and the public sphere generally, this being understood, however, as the successful outcome of women's own efforts.

One could even be tempted to see a convergence between East and West in a 'post-modern' return to traditional values and bonds of community, a perspective shared by groups within Polish sociology. In the process, however, it is forgotten that Eastern Europe does not question modernity ex post facto, but that it has recourse to pre-modern values and forms of integration which were not only perpetuated under the crust of the statist order, but which were also the analogy and support for the system, the structures of which were stabilised by forms of direct control, personal dependancies and the use of force, and which was pre-modern in this sense, irrespective of the claims it made for itself.

I should like to avail myself of a different approach to comparing East and West. In the more than ten years that I have lived in Poland, I have been shocked and dismayed by the deep lack of understanding for my feminist formulation of questions and my provocative ideas, considering the degree to which women are 'objectively' disadvantaged, but have also got to know and understand the position taken by my Polish women friends. The key to such understanding was not the ambivalence of a partial emancipation from above, nor was it attributable to any cultural peculiarities. It was rather a question of obtaining an insight into the fundamentally different social contexts in which women in East and West live.

I would like to discuss this context and its relevance for the perceptions and aspirations of women, by outlining below three paradigms of the women's movement in the West and then, in a second section, confronting these with three paradigms of the crisis in Eastern European societies. In a final section I shall then endeavour to answer the question posed in the title of this chapter.

One supposition underlying this approach to the question, 'Why is there no women's movement in Eastern Europe?' is that the origin of social movements is not to be explained in terms of a reflex reaction to 'objective' discrimination and disadvantage, but rather that the question must be asked as to the conditions under which the perception of deprivation occurs. To relate this to the women's movement, this means: under which conditions are the positions of men and women understood to be comparable? The idea of comparability presupposes equality.

My thesis is this: equality of the sexes can only refer to social existence and to existence that is perceived as social. Wherever society fails to act to achieve social integration, or is out of equilibrium, or still being struggled over – as is the case in Eastern Europe – 'man' and 'woman' cannot be conceived of as social roles and socially defined areas of experience, and thus neither can any awareness develop of the degree of deprivation that is present.

PARADIGMS OF THE WOMEN'S MOVEMENT

The women's movement is analysed in Western literature in terms of three paradigms:[3]

1. as the continuation of the Enlightenment, as the extension and materialisation of civil rights;
2. as a social movement embodying the reaction to the colonialisation of women's experience; and
3. as the critique of patriarchal sexual relations, which are revealed as the foundation of bourgeois society and its liberties, irrespective of formally equal rights.

1. The 'old' women's movement is viewed as the prosecution of the claim for civil rights by and for women. Here it was a matter of the admission of women to the public sphere on an equal basis to men. Having achieved formal civil rights, the material realisation of these rights then became the central demand raised by women, whereby the main focus was on equality of opportunity in the labour market. Developing out of this perspective, the private sphere was then taken up: the unequal division of domestic labour and the asymmetry of sexual relationships. The perspective of the public sphere implied the application to the family and marriage of concepts and values that were drawn from that sphere, aiming thus at their social regulation. Demands such as wages for housework, concepts such as 'emotional labour' (*Gefühlsarbeit*), or contractual insurance against the risks of marriage, all aimed at modelling the private sphere on the ideal of just exchange, and at projecting family and marriage as institutions which, corresponding to the model of democratic society, based solidarity on a community of interest, complementing it with the postulate of self-realisation and the autonomy of the individual.

This modernisation of interpersonal relationships harboured risks which were quickly recognised by women themselves. Rationalised interpersonal relationships were experienced as 'kaput', while the struggle for autonomy frequently led to isolation and loneliness. It was precisely this destabilisation of personal ties, and the devaluation of the individual and the feeling of insecurity accompanying it, that became a new source of conflict. One of the strongest impressions I had on my return to Germany was some graffiti painted on a garage door in Bremen: 'Scheiss-Beziehungskram' (roughly translatable as 'All this crappy relationship stuff').

2. The women's movement is characterised as an example of an *alternative social movement* reacting to the suffering that such colonialisation of the 'life world' (*Lebenswelt*) induces.[4] The penetration into interpersonal relationships of the standards of rationality of a system that is no longer integrated normatively through the agency of values, but rather through media such as money and formal law, is not only destructive in its effects in this sphere, but also deprives the system of its normative anchoring and motivational foundations. The 'new' women's movement responds to this problem in a defensive manner but cannot solve, in the estimation of Jürgen Habermas, the correctly perceived problem by further modernisation, owing to the traditionally romanticising and backward-looking quality of its categories and demands.[5]

The 'new' women's movement treats 'womanhood' as a culturally different mode of being, and no longer demands equal rights for equal individuals, but rather the right to womanhood and space for the articulation and realisation of the female identity. Corresponding to this is a new, higher valuation of the family and 'motherhood', but also tendencies towards self-imposed isolation, which are to be seen as the striving for space and shelter needed for the search for one's own identity.

In feminist theory the discovery of a 'female' morality has become a central theme of interest.[6] A 'female' morality is contrasted with a 'male' morality, the former relating to an ideal of responsibility, linked to concrete persons and oriented to contexts, as well as using inductive argumentation, the latter related to the ideal of the autonomous individual, oriented to norms and abstract principles, and using deductive argumentation. These moralities possess two correspondingly different concepts of solidarity. The autonomous 'male' individual subordinates himself to a form of solidarity that is to be institutionalised through the democratic formation of consensus with the aim of achieving a rational balance of interests, whereas, for the responsible 'female' individual, the integration of the individual into the network of bonds and obligations – solidarity – is part and parcel of human existence.

The demand that 'womanhood' be accorded its due recognition and place in society is, from the viewpoint of this perspective, no longer to be understood only as a *particular* interest of women, but as being in the general interest of society as a whole, advocated and supported by the women's movement.

3. This claim is theoretically founded and freed from any romanticising looking backwards under the paradigm of *patriarchal domination*.[7]

The distinction between 'male' and 'female' morality is not explained biologically or, as Gilligan does, psychologically (referring to the specificity of the mother–child relationship), but sociologically, and in two dimensions. Firstly, the formation of each of the two types of morality is attributed to gender-specific socialisation and life worlds. Womanhood is assigned the private, person-related sphere, while the public sphere, regulated through roles, is assigned to men. Secondly, the separation of the public and private spheres – including the gender-specific division of labour – is shown to be specific to bourgeois society, the freedom of the autonomous individual and the project of 'social solidarity' related to interests is, even in the conceptions of theoreticians, equated with motherliness and self-sacrifice on the part of women. This provides the guarantee for the socialisation and emotional stability of the male, strategically-acting autonomous individual.[8]

The transcendence of these patriarchal sexual relations is aimed, in the search for a new compromise, not only at the emancipation of women and men. By openly displaying the female ethics of responsibility as the reverse side of male instrumental reason, turning it into a social force in the process, the critique of patriarchy seeks to point out a theoretical alternative to the dialectics of enlightenment and to assist in establishing the project of a peaceful society.

PARADIGMS OF SYSTEMIC CRISIS AND SOCIAL MOVEMENTS IN EASTERN EUROPE

Three paradigms can also be distinguished for dealing with systemic crisis and social movements in Eastern Europe, with Poland and the Polish debate serving as our example here:[9]

1. the self-defence of society against the state and 'civil society';
2. the crisis of the statist order as the failure to regulate and integrate society; and
3. the collapse of the statist order.

1. The democratic opposition of the 1970s, and Solidarity during the 1980/1 period, consciously understood the formation of social movements as the *self-defence of society* against the totalitarian designs of the state.

The struggle for civil rights, the building of autonomous organisations and an unofficial and authentic public presence were to be conducted from their refuges; that is, the informal networks of family and friends, and the cultural values and memories that are lived out and handed down there. The aim of this strategy, namely to create a 'civil society' (by which was meant the rule of law, independent public opinion and media, freedom of association and, last but not least, parliamentary democracy), could not for tactical and strategic reasons be striven for by direct action against the political system, owing to Poland's geopolitical situation. In the thinking of J. Kuroń and A. Michnik, in particular, however, the amorphous social structure, itself a product of the centralisation of social relations in the state, was also a barrier to achieving political democracy. Social structures on which a pluralistic system could be established had first to be created. The strategy of the self-defence and self-organisation of society from below which characterised the policies of the opposition during the 1970s, and Solidarity in 1980/1, made allowance for this.

At the same time, more or less explicitly and consciously, a new model for 'civil society' was conceived of: the civil society to be constituted was envisaged as a society of people who were citizens, not owners of goods but *servants of society,* who constituted themselves not only as political but also as economic subjects in the project of socialising the state from below – including the socialisation of the centralised economy through self-administration. The displacement of 'civil society' from its economic basis and the social basis defined by it – private property and the exchange of goods – were not seen as problematic until the 1980s, and have proved only today to be a barrier to the conversion to political democracy.

2. In the social scientific analysis of the statist order and the social movements that were forming in opposition to it, the strict separation and opposition of 'society' and 'state' could not be upheld, nor could the assumption that there existed a clear initiative by society to defend itself.

Structural characteristics of the *system* – the lack of any differentiation between state, society and economy, and the form of direct domination (the non-formalised 'leading role of the Party') and personal control (the *nomenklatura*) – conditioned the weakness' of control exercised by a formally omnipotent centre. A form of *social integration*, described as 'phylogenetic' by the Polish sociologist W. Narojek, corresponded to rather than opposed these systemic structures, systemic techniques of integration and their inefficiency. The primary groups, circles of family and friends, and the moral norms and person-related loyalties that are lived out there, became the real and exclusive orientation for behaviour in a public order that was experienced as foreign and hostile, governed without rules or norms.[10]

Corresponding to this crisis of societal integration (*Vergesellschaftung*) was the dichotomy between 'us' and 'them', 'people' and 'institutions', 'society' and 'power', a dichotomy that signalled the moral rejection of the dominant order at the end of the 1970s, and out of which the strategy of the 'self-defence of society' against the state developed. The distinction between the world of people and the world of institutions as a separation of life spheres in consciousness is not to be equated with the differentiation between the private and public spheres in bourgeois society. It was not only the family that was projected as the alternative to the public institutions, but also the person as opposed to the role.

The 'retreat' into the private sphere therefore contains two elements: (1) a specific form of adaptation to the established order by repression of the social role in consciousness, a variety of schizophrenia in other words, and a personalising view of social relationships; (2) a real privatisation of the social role and instrumentalisation of position for private interests and private personal loyalties.

The lack of rationality on the part of the state organisations – the breaching of the legal regulatory system by *nomenklatura* and Party prerogative – were complemented from below by spontaneous processes of de-institutionalisation. The movement which opposed the state, and the process whereby social relations were being rendered increasingly anomic, established itself on the basis of pre-social identities and forms of integration: the cultural traditions and communities of family, networks of families, friends and circles of colleagues, and the national 'community of fate' as a 'confederation of families' (S. Nowak).

3.   An extension of the concept of systemic crisis as a crisis of societal integration is the paradigm of the *collapse of the statist order*.

In a different manner from the bourgeois revolutions, which released new structures which had already developed within the shell of the old order, the quasi-bourgeois revolutions in Eastern Europe reveal a social vacuum. There is a lack of economic subjects and structures, functioning institutions, social groups, crystallised and socially differentiated values, functioning rules and norms for living together socially. After the 'breakthrough' the new, democratically legitimised elites must therefore enter the state structures and check their accelerating collapse by building up social institutions.

It is no coincidence that during the 1980s there was a development of social scientific interest in the social reactions to the burdens caused by the German occupation of Poland.[11] The home and the family became at that time a microcosm for public opinion and communication, for production and the exchange of goods, this regression serving the physical survival of the people and the society. An analogous regression can be observed in the collapsing statist order. The increase in domestic production and the withdrawal to familial and friendship circles are an expression of this. Under the extreme pressure of the restructuring of society, which can only be viewed as a euphoric revolution from the distance of prosperous and functioning Western societies, but which for those affected signifies first and foremost a threat to all dimensions of their existence, this trend is sure to continue.

WHY IS THERE NO WOMEN'S MOVEMENT IN POLAND?

I should like to answer this question in three stages, corresponding to the three pairs of paradigms I have presented above:

1. with reference to the differences in significance that material equality and formal civil rights possess in East and West;
2. with reference to the lack of differentiation between the private and public sphere that explains the phenomena of a 'feminisation' of society; and
3. referring to the contrast between the overefficient modern societies in the West and collapsing social order in the East.

1. While the women's movement pushes for the material realisation of the formal equality of rights which is institutionalised in bourgeois society, the struggle in Poland is for the securing of *formal civil rights*. The old order was able, right up to the 1970s, to legitimise itself on the basis of material equality (of people, not primarily of the sexes), equality of opportunity and high mobility within certain limits. When the channels of mobility were closed during the 1970s and the resources for egalitarian social policies dried up, the deprivation in the political

sphere which had always been perceived became a central theme of conflict. By reforming the political system and suing for formal civil rights, the preconditions for the solution of material problems were to be created.

The political character of the mechanisms of social status assignment (distribution of income and career) was perceived as illegitimate, and in the process was translated into a demand for the removal of control over the economy by the state. The disadvantaged position of women, which was just as obvious and which studies had documented, did not need to be treated as a central problem within this context, in which the aim was to achieve a more efficient social system.[12]

Any questioning of existing sexual relations in the private sphere was blocked in that the processes of community formation (*Vergemein-schaftung*) which produced 'society' as a political subject, in the form of Solidarity, are founded on the basis of cultural tradition and the solidarity of the primary groups of family, friends and colleagues.

2.   The dichotomisation of the private and public sphere in consciousness hides in Poland the *lack of the differentiation between the private and the social sphere* that is typical for Western societies. The role of the state in the regulation of all social relationships coincides with the privatisation of roles within the state organisation.

This can explain phenomena which can be described as '*feminin-isation' of society*. By this is meant the orientation of men and women towards the family and the 'joys of family life'. Since the mid-1970s, studies on 'aims in life' have shown that a happy family life, recognition by the circle of friends, an adequate income and interesting work are to be found at the top of the hierarchy of values, and that high social position, social and political activity are not aims that are striven for.[13] Surveys among youth have shown that less than one per cent reject marriage as an insitution.[14]

Analyses of parental aims in raising their children show a low incidence of gender-specific qualities.[15] A dominance of 'female' context-related values was evident, however. Education objectives of conformism as opposed to self-control did not crystallise around 'obedience' and 'self-determination', but in the syndrome pair 'being a "good pupil"' and 'responsibility'. In addition, a second syndrome pair was discovered, in which the moral–political attitude to the system and morally interpreted choice between adaptation and withdrawal are articulated, where 'success' stood in a polar opposition to 'honesty' and 'ability to get along with other people'.

Investigations into prestige show that the esteem in which people are held derives primarily from characteristics of personality and manner of behaviour as experienced in direct social intercourse, and only secondly from aspects of the social status of the person concerned.[16]

These characteristics and their rankings do not demonstrate any gender-specific characteristics. What is more, it is 'female' qualities that are most prevalent here, too. For both men and women, the criteria for the esteem in which a person is held are, in the first place, a positive attitude to people, warmth, sincerity, willingness to help and to make sacrifices, collegiality and solidarity, while second place is occupied by care of the family, the home, the children and the welfare of the husband/wife. (These two sets of characteristics comprise 46.4 per cent of all answers referring to men, and 49 per cent of all answers referring to women.) Following these are industriousness, honesty, righteousness and readiness to help, and friendship. Particularly 'male' characteristics such as character and strength of will, staying power, specialist know-how, efficiency or ambition are named neither for men nor for women to any relevant extent. The criteria for the esteem in which a colleague is held show that loyalty and solidarity with other people, followed by work-related values, such as a sense of duty, discipline and ability to work with others, top the hierarchy of values – irrespective of whether the colleague in question was a man or a woman. As far as the esteem criteria for a person as a member of the family are concerned, there is what appears (at first glance) to be an analogous picture, in that care for the welfare of the family, the children and the husband/wife make up half of all named criteria. Below this surface of common family-centredness, however, a clear gender-specific division of labour prevails: the woman is expected to be a good housekeeper and to provide additional family income, while the man is expected to secure the material existence of the family and help with the housework.

Polish women (over 90 per cent of whom are gainfully employed) contribute 40–50 per cent of the family income.[17] The differing valuation of male and female employment is reflected in social reality in the fact that it is the woman that relegates her career aspirations to a position of secondary importance, in the interest of the familial obligations that both value so highly.[18] It is also the case, however, that the second job that the husband typically takes on to be able to make ends meet for the family frequently acts as a brake on career development in the narrower sense.

The orientation to family and friends that has been revealed says nothing about the actual frequency of contacts with friends, or about the functioning of the family.[19] What it does show, however, and that is the decisive aspect here, is that it is interpersonal relationships, and not social position and social role, that form the prism through which the individual sees his/her own person and social environment.

The following hypothetical conclusions concerning sexual relations and the identity of women can be drawn from this: the general orientation, characteristic of the entire society, towards 'female' values such as responsibility and person-related and community-related solidarity, family centrism and context-related perception, does not by any means exclude the disadvantaging of women, but it prevents a polarisation between 'male' and 'female' life worlds, values, mentalities and moralities, and the extent to which they are differently valued socially. The woman may be 'objectively' disadvantaged, but she does not experience this disadvantage as discrimination, or as exclusion from a 'man's world'.

The conflict relationship between men and women, as articulated by the women's movement in the West, is missing for yet another reason. It is a result of the perspective from within a certain social position: more precisely, the inequality of the sexes with respect to competition on the labour market and in the social sphere in the first place. This relationship of competition is the reason for a community of interest and an abstract solidarity among women based on this, which is expressed in the West in the form of spontaneous openness towards other women in general.

From the perspective of the private sphere, which is characteristic of East European society, the man appears to the woman as a potential partner and the woman as a competitor for the abstract man. There is thus no basis here for community of interest and abstract solidarity among women. Another thing that is missing is the openness, arising from any consciousness of a shared situation, towards the 'sister' one does not know. That again does not signify that there would be no room for practical solidarity with concrete women.

3.   The task in Western Europe is to forge links between the self-realisation of the autonomous individual and the social ethics of responsibility, particularly in view of an overeffective society that thoughtlessly uses up its own material, moral and social resources.[20] This problem is taken up and integrated in the patriarchy thesis. In Eastern Europe people are suffering under a failed experiment of modern times, the consequences of which are social and economic regressions that represent existential threats. It is not self-realisation but *security* that is becoming the dominant need, and in a destroyed society it is friends, marriage and family that offer such security.[21]

Surveys investigating what is considered to be the ideal marriage and family, or the ideal partner, demonstrate this clearly. Even school-children view the family as a closed solidaristic community, as a place of refuge and as an alternative to society. Solidarity appears to be more important than love. The ideal partner – girls and boys do not differ in their wishes in this respect – is supposed to provide support, security and repose.

The greater significance attached to the 'home' the increase in domestic production,[22] and the mental stress that women are more intensively exposed to than men, since care of the family is part of the woman's role,[23] imply an increased 'exploitation' of women. But what does such a term signify within the context of Polish society? Women in Poland – and in Eastern Europe generally – were never in their history the other side of the autonomous bourgeois individual, the side that safeguarded the necessary 'motherliness' for the development of that individual. Instead, they provided the backing and support for Polish freedom fighters. This liberation struggle was not related, however, to some idealised societal state in which, tacitly or explicitly, formally or informally, different standards applied for men and for women, and which for this reason were considered idealisations of 'male' freedom and rationality. The Polish liberation struggle was not and is not directed towards a utopian vision of society and an abstract concept of freedom, but rather the protection of the Polish home and a way of life that is understood as being common.[24]

Notes

1. See A. Bujwida (ed.), *Kobieta Polska lat osiemdziesiątych* (Warszawa:, 1988).
2. A small study from the 1980s among urban women established that, on being asked to decide between family and work, 45 per cent of the women asked opted for their family and only 20 per cent for their profession. What was interesting is that, within the first group, young women with secondary training and women in the age range of 31–40 years with university diplomas were over-represented. These women argued that, by giving more importance to their families, they prove to be wiser than their mothers. See M. Pomorska, 'Praca zawodowa i inne role społeczne kobiet', in A. Bujwida, *Kobieta Polska*, pp. 99–128.
3. See S. Kontos, 'Modernisierung der Subsumtionspolitik. Die Frauen-

bewegung in den Theorien neuer sozialer Bewegungen', in *Feministische Studien*, 1986/2 pp. 34–46.
4. See J. Habermas, *Theorie des kommunikativen Handelns* (Frankfurt:, 1985).
5. See also S. Kontos, 'Subsumtionspolitik', and the discussion on the paper of Elisabeth Conradi in *Feministische Studien*, 1989.
6. See C. Gilligan, *Die andere Stimme. Lebenskonflikte und Moral der Frau* (München/Zürich: 1984); A. Maihöfer, 'Ansätze zur Kritik des moralischen Universalismus. Zur moraltheoretischen Diskussion um Gilligans Thesen zu einer "weiblichen" Moralauffassung', in *Feministische Studien*, 1988/1, pp. 53–69.
7. See S. Kontos, 'Subsumtionspolitik'.
8. See M. Rumpf, 'Ein Erbe der Aufklärung. Imaginationen des "mütterlichen" in Max Horkheimers Schriften', in *Feministische Studien*, 1989/2, pp. 55–68.
9. See, for a more historical argumentation, M. Tatur 'Zur Dialektik der "civil society" in Polen', in R. Deppe, H. Dubiel and U. Rödel (eds), *Demokratischer Umbruch in Osteuropa* (Frankfurt:, 1990); M. Tatur, *Solidarność als Modernisierungsbewegung. Sozialstruktur und Konflikt in Polen* (Frankfurt:, 1989).
10. See W. Narojek, *Struktura społeczna w doświadczeniu jednostki* (Warszawa:, 1982).
11. See P. Łukasiewicz, 'Funkcja domu w okresie okupacji Niemieckiej', in *Kultura i Społeczeństwo*, 1989/2, pp. 67–82.
12. See H. Domański, 'Zasady rekrutacji do stanowisk kierowniczych', in *Stud. Soc.*, 1986/3, pp. 155–78; H. Domański, 'Dystrybucji dochodów w odziałach gospodarki', in *Stud. Soc.*, 1985/1, pp. 219–40.
13. Again proved by E. Nasalska, Z. Sawiński, 'Przemiany celów i dazeń zyciowych społeczeństwa polskiego w latach 1977–1986, in *Kultura i Społeczeństwo*, 1989/1, pp. 169–83.
14. See *Młode pokolenie czasu kryzysu i reform. Polska Młodzież 87* (Warszawa:, 1988) p. 48.
15. See J. Koralewicz-Zębik, 'Wartości rodzicielskie a stratyfikacja społeczna', in *Stud. Soc.*, 1982/3–4, pp. 237–62.
16. See I. Reszke, *Prestiz'u zawodów i osób* (Wrocław:, 1984).
17. This figure is given by A. Bujwida, *Kobieta Polska*, p. 13, taking into account the markedly lower incomes of women it seems very high.
18. See E. Tarkowska, 'Zróznicowanie stylów z'ycia w Polsce: pokolenie i płeć', in *Kultura i Społeczeństwo*, 1985/2, pp. 55–73.
19. As an international survey of contacts in Eastern Europe [shows] – Hungary being the example here – they are not necessarily more frequent. But they seem to have a greater importance; see F. Höllinger, 'Familie und soziale Netzwerke in fortgeschrittenen Industriegesellschaften', in *Soziale Welt*, 1989/4, pp. 512–37.
20. I am referring here to J. Berger, 'Modernitätsbegriffe und Modernitäskritik in der Soziologie', in *Soziale Welt*, 1988/3, pp. 224–36.
21. See H. Swida, 'Młodzież licealna schyldu lat 70', in J. Koralewicz-Zębik (ed.), *Społeczeństwo polskie przed kryzysem w świetle badań socjologicznych z lat 1977–1979* (Warszawa: 1987) pp. 183–224.

22. See A. Wiśniewski, 'Gospodarstwo domowe wobec kryzysu', in I. Pałaszewska-Reimdel (ed.), *Polskie gospodarstwa domowe życie codzienne w kryzysu* (Warszawa, 1986) pp. 218–30.

23. See CBOS, *Kondycja psychiczna Polaków w 1989*, Kommunikat z badań, Serwis informacyjny 1/1990, CBOS Warszawa.

24. The pragmatic and defensive approach to the project of a 'civil society' in Poland I point out in M. Tatur, 'Zur Dialektik'.

4 From Closed to Open Communication System: New Information and Communication Technologies and the Rebirth of Civil Society in Communist Eastern Europe

Tomasz Goban-Klas and
Teresa Sasinska-Klas

In that process of change the loss of Communist monopoly over mass communications was the key to the breakdown of Communism totalitarianism. (Zbigniew Brzezinksi, *The Grand Failure. The Birth and Death of Communism in the Twentieth Century*, 1989, p. 254)

THE SYSTEM THAT STALIN BUILT

Soviet communism was, from its very beginning, totalitarian in its nature, exercising threefold control: over politics, over economy, and over ideology (including that over the media of communication). In a communist country the rulers were indeed 'three in one': politicians, managers and priests. Thus the general secretary of the Communist Party of the Soviet Union since Lenin's time was the supreme leader, supreme manager and supreme priest, all in one person.

Of this threefold hold over society, the control over ideology (in practice over the media) was considered to be crucial. Marxism–Leninism was a compulsory official belief and the cornerstone of communist society. It was Lenin in the early 1920s, who theoretically developed that perspective and carried it out in practice. Lenin, once

76

a champion of the free press, when it served the Bolsheviks in their struggle against the Tsarist regime, and later against the Provisional Government, became a promoter of strict control and eventually of monopoly of the press shortly after the October Revolution. However he at least left some freedom to his fellow-Bolsheviks, while denying it to all other parties.

It was Stalin who, following the internal logic of dictatorship, took one further step, and set up one-man rule, not only in politics, but in the media as well. Since the 1930s, he had been successfully building an almost perfect 'closed' society, to use Karl Popper's concept,[1] and an even more closed communication system. While Lenin, at least, preached *glasnost'* as a means to tame notorious Russian bureaucrats, Stalin made '*Ne-glasnost*'', or secrecy, the basic tenet of his rule and of the Soviet state in general.

In the early 1930s, Stalin introduced the system of limiting not only the flow of information by cutting off contacts with foreigners, but also the mobility of his own subjects, the Soviet citizens. Internal passports (or ID cards) were withdrawn from peasants, chaining them to their collective farms. He limited travel between republics, extended forbidden zones, not only to foreigners, but even to the Russians. Borders were closed; thus even travel to 'fraternal socialist countries' was, for a private person, practically impossible.[2] Maps of Moscow were not to be published – and when they eventually appeared in the early 1980s, they gave false distances and shapes! Telephone directories were considered unnecessary. Stalin kept information secret even from his closest collaborators, like Nikita S. Khrushchev, at that time the first secretary of the Moscow communist party organisation and a Politbureau member. Khrushchev complained later, in his memoirs published in the West, that he had no access to vital information; indeed, he was not allowed to inquire into issues beyond his own sphere of responsibility. Therefore even he, if we believe him, did not realise the full scale of terror.

Stalin kept communication separated and preferably vertical, limiting and hindering horizontal ones as much as he could. He ruled by fear and by ignorance, sustaining a state-of-siege model of propaganda. In 1941, three days after the German invasion of the Soviet Union, a decree by the Soviet government made it compulsory for citizens to deliver to the police not only any radio transmitters (which was understandable at the time), but in addition all standard radio sets.[3] It became obvious that the authorities were afraid that their own subjects could learn something inappropriate from foreign broadcasts.

Just after his victory over Nazi Germany, when the whole world admired 'Uncle Joe' as the courageous generalissimo, Stalin ordered thousands of his brave and dedicated soldiers to be shipped to the Gulag archipelago, to labour camps, simply because they had the misfortune to have been captured by Germans, even for a few days or hours, they were labelled traitors and cowards, and as such were deserving of severe punishment. That was an official reason. In fact the true reason was that they had learned more than the official propaganda. Stalin was afraid of information about Western prosperity, which they might be willing to disseminate, even if the prosperity was that which they had seen in Poland during the war.

The former, communist, mass media system in Eastern Europe had a very simple and well-defined structure. Everything there was to be planned, although this was a wish rather than a reality. At the same time it was organised as a monopoly – again more of a wish than a reality. Setting up the press on the basis of such a plan was made possible, of course, by the absence of private enterprise and the concentration of power and authority in the hands of the communist party.[4]

The mass media system was then very logical as it had a well-described set of assumptions, albeit some based on hidden ideological premises, and the political practice favoured only one of them, that of the supremacy of the decisions of the central governing body. The ideology of the mass media was called 'Lenin's theory of the press of the new type'. Its constituent elements were such principles as *partiinost'* or party-mindedness, high ideological content, a 'link with life' and so on. From the theoretical point of view, it was a closed system, based on controlled vertical information flow, limiting as much as possible any horizontal and spontaneous connections. It did not allow any spontaneity, any new ideas, uncontrolled by the party. Thus it was doomed to stagnation, despite its initial, revolutionary dynamics. Thus the Brezhnev years were rightly called the 'era of stagnation', while in the West there was in train a true information revolution.

THE BIRTH OF INDEPENDENT COMMUNICATION

But if there has not been any information revolution in the Soviet Union, at the top or one initiated from above, in politics, industry, trade, agriculture, or science, there has been a continuing revolution in communication between people, and that not since Gorbachev, but since Stalin's death. As Zbigniew Brzezinski put it:

Under the conditions of communism and particularly in the setting of its intense and monopolistic indoctrination, the following process takes place. An ideologically alienated mass is created, eager to ingest alternative information. It thus seizes upon new techniques of mass communications – such as foreign radios, television, video cassettes, underground press – to forge a dissenting if vague political outlook. Economic failures enable politically active intellectuals to transform that outlook into demands not only for socioeconomic but also for political pluralism and for the rule of law.[5]

It seems appropriate here to point out that, from its very beginnings the communist party cleverly and innovatively used the power of the mass media. Lenin's Bolshevik party used 'underground', that is illegal, publications to advance the cause of revolution. Later Lenin supported, by all accessible means, the readership of the Bolshevik press. He was also an enthusiast of radio and film documentaries. He did not spare expense on propaganda at times when famine and misery in Russia reached unprecedented proportions; he ordered the use of Russian gold reserves to finance internal and external propaganda campaigns.[6]

Although with television the Soviets were a bit slower, in the late 1960s a crash programme increased the production of TV sets so that now fully 93 per cent of the population can watch television programmes, sometimes relayed by a complex satellite network.[7] Telecommunications have been improved with satellite systems. But here their successes stops. It is enough to say that in the Soviet Union computers, microelectronics, and similar devices are still far below Western standards. Let a joke make the point: 'In the Soviet Union – boasted a factory manager – we produce not semi-conductors, but full conductors, and our chips are the biggest in the world!' The information revolution has not yet penetrated the Soviet Union, at least, on a mass and profitable level.

However the populations of communist countries have always been more curious, more open to innovation then the leadership. So they have looked for any alternative information they could get. The first signs of change appeared soon after the death of Stalin. Lavrenti Beria, head of the Soviet security services, and the closest collaborator of the dictator, possibly his designated successor, was removed from office, and eventually tried and shot. The mild 'thaw',[8] or the Soviet spring, had begun, and reached its peaks in 1956 and 1964, the years of the XXth and XXIIth Congresses of the Communist Party of the Soviet Union. These events naturally had repercussions in the 'fraternal socialist countries', especially in Hungary and Poland, where popular revolts occurred.

In the early 1950s, in the period of the Cold War, the United States, following its policy as 'champion of the free world', had set up two radio stations broadcasting to the 'captive nations' of Eastern Europe: Radio Liberty and Radio Free Europe (in Munich).[9] Of course the communist authorities were not happy at all with them, and used all available means to discourage their subjects from listening, jamming being the most effective. But even that was not foolproof. Those more interested in politics always managed to sift information from the accompanying noise.

So when, in 1954, afraid of suffering Beria's fate, a senior Polish security official escaped to the West, his revelations about mass terror and fabricated political trials of the former communist leaders, were broadcast on the waves of Radio Free Europe (RFE). They had an enormous impact on political life in the country, partly because most listeners were party members and lived in Warsaw. These broadcasts, if they did not directly cause ferment in the ranks of the communist party and, in particular, amongst the communist youth, at least fuelled it. This, of course, is not an example of the power of radio, rather of the power of truth. Radio was in this case a medium, not a message. Since that time, foreign transmissions, not exclusively from Radio Liberty or Radio Free Europe but also the BBC World Service, Deutsche Welle, Radio France Internationale, broadcasting in vernacular languages, were continually present in Eastern Europe, affecting the knowledge and attitudes of its inhabitants. In the long run, they played their role well, although occasionally, as during the Hungarian uprising of 1956, they created false expectations of possible help on the part of Western powers.[10]

To a lesser extent the same might be said of television. It has always been a pro-government medium, but it has also carried a certain amount of visual information which was not fully controlled: in news bulletins, in newsreels, and especially in foreign mini-series and movies. However the true television revolution began when, thanks to improvements in reception, more and more people could start watching their neighbours' televisions.

If foreign radio was the first independent medium of mass communication in the communist countries, independent, 'underground' publications were the second. They were even more important in building a diverse opposition and, finally, helping to bring about the final collapse of communism.

Paradoxically the first theory of the role of an independent, underground press in building a 'second' society, could be found in the writing of ... Lenin. It was he who, in his article 'What is to be done' (1902) stressed the role which illegal newspapers play not only in propaganda and agitation, but in organisation of the party as well.[11] His idea was simple: participation, in any form, in the production and dissemination of illegal publications encouraged participation in oppositional activity, helped recruit party members and formed party cadres.

A more elaborate approach to the role of the press was developed in the 1970s in communist countries when strict communist (or, better to say, Stalinist) rule eased, but the system still remained totalitarian in nature. It did not allow any spontaneous, autonomous activity on the social level, and still considered any tendency towards such activity illegal. The natural inclination of individuals was to resist the artificial, inhuman, and (most important) inefficient system of state control by developing independent activities.

No wonder that the concept of an independent society emerged as a reinterpretation of the relation of the state to civil society.[12] It stressed the need to restore a civil society in Eastern Europe, characterised by legality, human rights and freedoms, the revival of the public sphere and public opinion, plurality and common action. In this perspective the state (totalitarian) and civil society were counterpoised.[13]

The term *samizdat* has been defined briefly as 'typewritten copies, transferred by hand', and, more adequately, as 'unapproved material reproduced unofficially ... by hand, typewriter, mimeograph or occasionally by xerography'.[14]

Such independent printing, born of the urge to overcome governmental control, appeared during the late 1950s in the Soviet Union.[15] At first it was exactly what the word means: the term *samizdat*, used by a Moscow poet as an ironic parody of such official acronyms as *Gosizdat*, meaning State Publishers (short for *Gos*udarstvennoe *Izdat*elstvo), was an abbreviation of the description of the bound, typewritten publication of his poems, *Samsebyaizdat*, that is, Do-it-Yourself Press.[16]

These humble beginnings[17] led in the 1960s and 1970s to what was virtually a second literary system.[18] After the Soviet Union, *samizdat* developed in Czechoslovakia, where it was perfected at least in form, if not content. There is no room here to describe those independent presses. Although their production was a very impressive, considering the police prosecution of such activities, they of course could not compete, in terms of the size of readership, with official publications. Not everyone read these publications; not everyone was interested in them. Nevertheless, as Mianowicz wrote, they broke 'the Communist state monopoly of information'.[19] What was perhaps more important, they created the cadres ready to take power when the occasion arose, as happened with Havel in Czechoslovakia and with the Solidarity leaders in Poland.

TECHNOLOGIES OF FREEDOM

Another mortal enemy of the government monopoly of television is the video. In countries with state-controlled media it brings freedom of choice. It allows people to enrich their meagre television diet, especially in the Soviet Union, when the choice has been restricted mainly to domestic movies. Government propaganda is always dull and video brings a new, colourful, rich Hollywood world into homes.

Moreover video, in the form of the camcorder, is used to produce visual documentaries of events that government television cannot or does not want to cover. This happened in the case of an amateurish videotape of demonstrations in Tibilisi, Georgia, in May 1989, when several young women were killed. That videotape, shown first on Western television and later on Soviet screens, caused Parliament to demand explanations from the police, a thing unheard of before.

The video, in the form of the camcorder, is an example of so-called new information and communication technologies, or new media. Here there are many technological inventions, such as computers, copiers, fax, laser printers, satellite television and so on. Their adaptation by dissidents, and by the citizenry at large, in comparison with the snail's pace of their implementation by official structures, has been extraordinarily fast, especially in recent years. Thus, in Eastern Europe, more and more satellite dish antennas can be seen, especially in Hungary and Poland.

Underground publishers in Poland were quick to catch up with new technology and to use desktop software and laser printers to improve and increase their output. No wonder that the first independent, post-communist Polish daily, *Gazeta Wyborcza*, set up in May 1989, was composed on MacIntosh computers. It recently launched an English international edition, a move facilitated by the use of computer word processing and desktop publishing.

Fax machines are catching on fast, but, for obvious reasons, they are used almost exclusively by institutions, not private citizens. It is, however, worth mentioning here that, during the Chinese students' revolt in June 1989, fax machines were widely used on campuses to send messages abroad, and later to receive messages of support, students thus keeping in touch with world public opinion.

Other new means of communications were also important for spontaneous horizontal communication as with, for instance, electric-powered portable megaphones used during demonstrations. An automatic long-distance dialling system allowed Radio Free Europe to call well-known dissidents in Poland during a wave of strikes in May 1988 and to broadcast those conversations live. This has become standard practice for RFE, transforming it into a second, alternative radio network in Poland.

Let us pass on to analysis of the social facets of the information revolution.

In the spirit of detente in the 1970s, the spirit of Helsinki, communists could no longer, and did not want, to control all knowledge, all behaviour, all fashion, all art. Reluctantly the authorities reconciled themselves to new currents. Thus the emergence of counter-culture was connected with some forms of information flow – somehow new ideas, pictures, habits found their way through the Iron Curtain. Therefore in Moscow or Leningrad, in Budapest and Pecs, thousands of young converts to various forms of experience appeared. They ranged from old-fashioned, old-style hippies, to Hare Krishna, punks and skinheads. Official attitudes were initially very reluctant, later becoming more tolerant, but even those who were for banning such manifestations admitted that this had become virtually impossible since the invention of the tape-recorder.

Thus, apart from *samizdat*, *magnizdat* appeared; that is, illegally produced and distributed audio and video tapes. In Poland there was even a 'spoken newspaper', in the form of an audio-cassette, circulated as a weekly publication. In the Soviet Union there developed the phenomenon of Vladimir Vysotsky, an idolised singer, who, although widely known, had only two of his tapes officially published as records by the Soviet record company, 'Melodiya'. That particular mixture, youth and the tape-recorder, had become very explosive.

What we have seen recently, especially in Czechoslovakia, Romania and East Germany, and to a lesser extent in Poland and in the Soviet Union, has been a revolt of young people, mostly students, as in Czechoslovakia, or youth, as in East Germany, or simply kids, as in Romania. They became 'a new avantgarde', to adapt an old communist term, who, like the proletariat in Marx's vision, had nothing to lose but their chains. They had seen the other world, on Western television, or on video, and they liked what they saw.

The examples of the new technologies, whether tape-recorders, short-wave radio sets or videos, have been used by reform-minded journalists, social scientists and even politicians to promote an idea of profound changes in information policy, in short a policy of *glasnost'*. Let me quote only one of them, Felix Dymov, who in an article 'What is not Forbidden is Allowed', published in the Soviet literary weekly, *Literaturnaya Rossiya*, in June 1988, put it this way:

> there is a fear on the part of Communist officials of losing the monopoly on information. Yet the state has announced an overall programme of computerisation, which cannot but lead to the loss of this monopoly. The appearance of tape-recorders means a loss of governmental control over what people hear. With videos it practically loses control over what people see. With computers ... control will be lost over what people read.

Glasnost' policy is now adapting to new technologies. Recent Soviet changes in this respect include the following:

- in September 1988, custom duties on individual imports of personal computers, printers and video equipment were drastically reduced or eliminated;
- in November 1988, the Soviet Union stopped jamming Radio Liberty, Deutsche Welle and Kol Israel;
- in April 1989, it was stated on a television news programme that Soviet-made satellite dish antenas would go on sale to the general public;
- in May 1989, it was announced that an agreement with Ted Turner's CNN Network had been concluded, and that programmes would be available to organisations and individuals through a cable service.
- from 1991 Russian Radio has carried regular broadcasts from the BBC World Service.

There is still a long road to tread to the information revolution, and an even longer one to the information society, but first steps have been taken. Thus the Soviet reformers and policy makers are fully aware of what technological change brings about. At the same time, youth becomes frustrated and alienated from the system. This happened almost simultaneously in all Eastern European countries. Undoubtedly information not only facilitated recent change, it was a necessary ingredient of it. This view is supported by a number of observations.

First, Despite all efforts by communist governments to keep control over all information and communication lines, a task which could only partially be carried out, even with the use of mass terror and repression, control was gradually lost and new, non-controlled information started to pour in. This was dangerous both for ideology and for the system.

Second, we live in an information-rich environment, both in the West and in the East. Stalin's legacy of paranoic secrecy, playing everything close to the chest, simply could not survive any longer. Third, and most important, the Eastern European systems have been characterised by the dominance of politics over the economy. Revolution by information therefore happened mainly in the political dimension. Even the dissidents now in power in Poland and Czechoslovakia understand information and communication from a political, rather than an economic point of view. Therefore there is still a long road to a developed and economically sound information sector.

THE NEW LANDSCAPE OF THE MASS MEDIA IN EASTERN EUROPE

The present landscape of the mass media in Eastern Europe is so different from what it was quite recently that it would shock any observer. At the beginning of 1989, in four countries in the region – the GDR, Czechoslovakia, Bulgaria and Romania – the system was till typically communist. The situation in the Soviet Union was slightly different, owing to the new information policy known as *glasnost'*, but much of that difference lay in the content of the media, rather than in its organisation. The structure of the media was basically the same as, say, ten years before. So there was only liberalisation and the relaxation of media control, and not freedom of the press, in the Soviet Union.

Only Poland and Hungary could boast different mass media systems. Hungary had some experience of independent publishing and, characteristically, of the first intrusion of Western capital in the world of Eastern Europe – that of the weekly *Reform*, in which Axel Springer has

49 per cent of shares. In Hungary, between June and October 1989, some 220 new publications were registered, nearly two-thirds of them Budapest-based.

In Poland, at the beginning of the year, the situation was even more remote from the classical communist model. Besides the flourishing underground press, the first Polish private periodical *Respublica* was set up in 1988. In April 1989 the 'Round Table Agreement' allowed an independent, private, 'Solidarity'-oriented, mass-circulation daily to appear, *Gazeta Wyborcza*. The new, non-communist government, elected in August 1990, promised the removal of censorship, which in fact had already ceased to operate. Instead of jamming, the state radio and television began to collaborate with foreign stations. In Cracow – following the example of Warsaw with Soviet television – the Italian television channel, *Rai Uno*, began to rebroadcast its programmes. Also the first private FM radio began to broadcast.

Poland led the transformation of the media, but even in Poland the broadening scope and range of journalistic freedom was due mainly to political changes, rather than structural changes in the media system. Until 1991 the government could not decide to break with its monopoly over television and radio.

The same may be said about the other East European countries after their political emancipation. The change of political system in the GDR, in Czechoslovakia and in Romania during the 'Autumn of the People' of 1989 were supported by the media, but the legal regulations, economic conditions, personnel and audiences remained basically the same for a long time after the rejection of the communist system. So the direction of the change in the mass media remains unknown and undetermined.

In Poland the first element of the media system to be changed was the press. It was dominated by the RSW 'Prasa-Książka-Ruch', the publishing institution which printed almost all Polish dailies, about one-half of weeklies, all illustrated magazines and had the monopoly of newspaper distribution. RSW was owned by the Communist party, which drew from it most of the money for its expenses. This huge, profit-oriented, ideological concern, enjoying a quasi-monopolistic position, was dissolved in March 1990 by decision of Parliament. It is now in the process of reorganisation, privatisation and so on. Nobody really knows what will be the outcome. For the time being, some publications, especially those in the red, have disappeared, but the main changes have been in personnel – many editors-in-chief were fired; new ones, usually with a background in the opposition were nominated.

There is no clear idea of what to do with the RSW legacy. At first there was a tendency, contained in the law demanding the dissolution of the RSW, that it should be separated into publishing co-operatives, but this solution looked economically unsound and socially unjust, in the sense that old journalistic teams and editorial boards, would thus be privileged. There was talk of creating many smaller press chains, with some foreign capital (limited to 20 per cent) and, most probably, with government control through ownership of over 50 per cent of shares.

Censorship in Poland finally ended on 6 June 1990. It was perhaps not the most severe but the best known among Eastern European countries, owing to the escape of the Polish censor to the West in 1977. The jamming of foreign radios stopped in 1988. In September 1989, the most notorious of them, Radio Free Europe, opened an office in Budapest. On 24 May 1990, it did the same in Prague, and one day later in Warsaw.

The most interesting development, however, is the growing number of special-interest publications and small presses. Here we have a great number of sensational magazines (called *Detective*, *Reporter* and so on), comics, erotic magazines (like *Natura*), computer magazines, gay magazines, illustrated magazines (like *Success* and *Bon Voyage*), sports magazines, tennis, skiing – even TV-satellite guides.

There are new types of commercials, full-page foreeign. Even commercials selling shares, and as *Universal* or *Drewbud*, are offered. On television there are more and more commercials, usually offering very expensive goods and products. The main obstacle to the development of the press in Poland is the poor performance of the national economy, the deep recession and the high price of newsprint (the price rose by nearly 500 per cent in January 1990).

CONCLUSIONS: COMMUNICATIONS AT THE CROSSROADS

In Poland there is freedom of the press, in terms of the absence of censorship, but there is not – or is not seen, in the present and near future at least – independence of the media, in the sense of Western journalism. Most of the press is still dependent on the arbitrary decision of the governmental Liquidation Commission on the RSW 'Prasa'. The newly-established periodicals are very weak in terms of financing and readership. The advertising market is limited. Radio and television are still the property of the state and under full government control. There is little understanding of the value of journalistic independence, credibility and so on. Rather, new parties and organisations complain about their own poor image in the mass media and would like to take control over them. The road to independence will be long and crooked.

The same could be said of the situation in other Eastern European countries. Adaption to pluralism and democracy is not easy: 'In Romania today no one understands the role of an independent, critical press.' As Jim Podesta, an American who opened a short-lived School of Journalism for 20 students in Bucharest, said: 'Essentially there is no journalism here. Opinion is news. Facts are dispensable.'[20]

Opening up East European media to the competition of ideas offers the Western media the chance to enter. For the moment the introduction of Western influences is openly commercial and limited. In future it could mean the introduction of Western commercial culture and political intervention. One dangerous situation seems to be in the Hungarian media, where Axel Springer has already bought four county newspapers. A Reuter report on 23 May 1990 said that Springer had acquired control of '6 regional dailies, 5 weeklies, 10 local papers and 40 other titles.'[21] Robert Maxwell acquired a 40 per cent share in the *Magyar Hirlap*, printing 100 000 copies.

Thus, in the opinion of many observers, the general if uneven movement towards Western standards of objectivity, responsibility and pluralism in the media is hindered by the persistence of old habits, traditions and structures; by journalists used to old ways and unconformable to the new; and by the lack of professional experience or equipment.[22]

It will be just as difficult, and perhaps as courageous, to build a normal society and normal media as it was to develop a 'second' society and a 'second' media.

Notes

1. Karl Popper, *The Open Society and Its Enemies* (London: Routledge, 1945).
2. Robert Conquest (ed.), *The Politics of Ideas in the USSR* (New York: Praeger, 1967).
3. Note that a similar decree was issued in Poland in the autumn of 1939, not, however, by the Polish government, but by the Nazi occupation administration.

4. Alex Inkeles, *Public Opinion in Soviet Russia. A Study in Mass Persuasion* (Cambridge, Mass.: Harvard University Press, 1950) p. 143.
5. Z. Brzezinski, *The Grand Failure. The Birth and Death of Communism in the Twentieth Century* (New York: Charles Scribner, 1989) pp. 254–5.
6. In 1922, a most powerful radio station, Commintern (Communist International) was built in Moscow and began to transmit its messages. In the 1930s, the Soviets were the first to start broadcasting to foreign countries on a massive scale, an activity that suited their ideology of spreading the revolutionary ideal throughout the world: Vadim Medish, *The Soviet Union* (New Jersey: Prentice-Hall, 1984) p. 221.
7. Ellen Mickiewicz, *Split Signals. Television and Politics in the Soviet Union* (Oxford: Oxford University Press, 1989).
8. To use the title of Ilya Ehrenburg's book of 1954.
9. Robert T. Holt, *Radio Free Europe* (Minneapolis: University of Minnesota Press, 1958).
10. Ibid.
11. *Lenin about the Press* (Prague: International Organization of Journalists, 1972) pp. 190–9.
12. The concept of 'civil society' was developed by Locke, Hegel, de Tocqueville and Marx. It was applied to Polish 'dissent' in the 1970s by Jacques Rupnik, in his article, 'Dissent in Poland: 1968–78, in Rudolf Tokes (ed.), *Opposition in Eastern Europe* (London: Macmillan, 1979) ch. 6.
13. Zbigniew Pelczynski, 'Solidarity and the Re-birth of Civil Society in Poland', in John Keane (ed.), *Civil Society and the State, New European Perspectives* (London: Verso, 1988).
14. D. Pospielovsky, 'From Gosizdat to Samizdat and Tamizdat', *Canadian Slavonic Papers*, XX, no. 1 (March 1978) p.44.
15. In fact, samizdat is nothing more that the revival of the methods used by the opponents of Stalin in the 1920s and even the 1930s. After the left-wing Opposition was denied printing facilities it tried to disseminate its material 'from hand to hand'. This 'illegal' printing and circulation was one of the charges levelled against it in the 1930s. See George Sanders, (ed.), *Samizdat. Voices of the Soviet Opposition* (New York: Monad Press, 1974) pp. 7–8.
16. H. G. Skilling, *Samizdat and an Independent Society in Central and Eastern Europe* (London: Macmillan, 1989) pp. 4–5.
17. Although it should be stressed that illegal publications had a long history in Russia and Eastern Europe. In 1790, a book of A. Radishchev, *A Journey from Petersburg to Moscow*, after being banned by the authorities, was passed around in manuscript form among Russian readers. The famous Russian poets, Pushkin and Griboyedov, circulated their manuscripts privately. In the 1920s, the typewritten works of Osip Mandelshtam, especially his an anti-Stalin poem, were passed around in what was then called 'Underwood', after the typewriter used. See further in Gordon Skilling, *Samizdat*, pp. 3–4.
18. According to estimates, the various types of dissident documents in the Soviet Union were found to number 47 items in 1965; that figure doubled in 1966, and doubled again in 1968. The grand total over the first decade

(1964–74) was about 2000. F.J.M. Feldbrugge, *Samizdat and Political Dissent in the Soviet Union* (Leyden: Sijthoff & Noordhoff, 1975) p. 12.

19.   Tomasz Mianowicz, 'Unofficial publishing lives on', *Index on Censorship*, 12, No. 2 (April 1983) p. 25.

20.   Quote from Kevin Devlin, 'Postrevolutionary Ferment in the East European Media', *Report on Eastern Europe*, RFE, Vol. 1, No. 28, 13 July 1990, p. 51.

21.   Ibid., p. 52.

22.   Ibid., p. 53.

5 Economic Change and Civil Society in Poland
Witold Morawski

INTRODUCTION

The aim of this introduction is to show the range of possible relationships between economic change and civil society. Although I concentrate my attention on Poland in the 1980s when the nexus between the two phenomena became clearly visible, I shall begin with a characterisation of attempts made by the political authorities to carry out economic reforms in the pre-Solidarity period. My point is that these changes were doomed to failure because the power centre was not able to get social support for them. The characteristic feature of the period was the absence of civil society. In effect these changes did not deserve to be called 'economic changes', but were rather reorganisations or false reforms. They happened to be made under the slogan of 'economic decentralisation', outlined in the next section.

The involvement of society in the economic reforms grew with the creation of Solidarity in 1980. It could be seen as the embryo of civil society in the workplace; that is, an institution of self-organisation of employee's interests and values independent of the state. This initial involvement was interrupted by the introduction of martial law and, in general, by political problems which seemed to be even more urgent for the society than economic ones. Hence civil society and its manifestations, like underground Solidarity, samizdat-type press, self-defence groups, emerging political clubs, self-management bodies and so on, functioned for nearly a decade either under the guise of anti-state phenomena,[1] or as substitutes for politics (see third section).

The events of 1989, including the round-table talks, the partially free parliamentary elections, the formation of the first non-communist government in the Soviet bloc, and also the prolonged economic crisis, led to a shift of focus from social–political issues to economic change. The latter had to be urgently initiated by the government using the whole machinery of the existing state. At such an historic moment civil society could no longer function as an anti-state force. Open opposition to the state in general had to be replaced by opposition directed just at the socialist state. This being so, there was a need to develop a post-socialist state ideal. In fact Solidarity had developed such an idea earlier under the name of the 'self-governing republic' (fourth section), but the first steps of the new government showed that other visions had also existed within the Solidarity movement.

By the beginning of the 1990s people have come to the conclusion that successful transitions to markets and democracy have to meet many difficult conditions. They are often summed up in the idea of 'a mature civil society'. Opinions on how to achieve it are differentiated. Economists seem to be divided. For the triumphant neo-liberals marketisation and privatisation should be realised quickly, even if it requires shock therapy for the society. For social–democratic forces a more gradual strategy would not only be more humane, but also more realistic. Political scientists formulate their own expectations concerning a viable political system: the role of parties, parliament, government, public opinion and so on. Sociologists speak about large middle classes and the rest. This panorama of requirements suggests that civil society can be seen under the guise of the pre-state, as examined in the fifth section. How this could be met in the economic sphere is discussed in more detail in the section that follows.

As we can see, the relationship between the economic change and the civil society has undergone an evolution in Poland. The sources of this evolution are located not just in the economy or in society, but also in politics. Linkages between these three seem to be of crucial importance. In the past they were linked negatively, forming a sort of 'vicious circle'. Now there is a chance of transforming these linkages into positive ones, but the problem is how to achieve this. In my opinion, it requires first of all finding an optimum balance between the autonomy and dependency of these structures; more precisely, practical ways of securing relative autonomy for all of them (see the conclusion to this chapter).

DECENTRALISATION REFORMS IN THE ABSENCE OF CIVIL SOCIETY

The Polish economy has been subjected to more or less intensive reform since the middle of the 1950s.[2] The first two major reforms had the aim of decentralisation: the reform after 1956 (which also introduced elements of social participation) and the reform after 1970.

According to the diagnosis of the authors of decentralising conceptions, the main source of the sickness of the system was the direct centralisation of decisions; this produced more and more errors as the economic system became ever more complex with economic growth. In this situation the therapy ought to be to move decisions from the highest and higher levels to the middle and lower ones – or even better to the enterprise itself. The quantitative reduction of commands coming from the top was supposed to be accompanied by a qualitative change: direct decisions were supposed to be replaced by parametric instruments (prices, taxes, credits and so on).

Both diagnosis and therapy could be regarded as correct, but at the same time superficial. The superficiality consisted in the tacit assumption that the economy could be run from the top. Lenin himself compared the whole economy to one big factory or post office. In a nutshell, the economy is perceived as a part of the administrative structure of the state. In fact the idea of decentralisation assumed the replacement of direct with indirect centralisation. The assumption was that the state is capable of making the best decisions concerning:

1. The economy: the state can do this without relying on market mechanisms. In the Marxist tradition (though not all of it) the desire exists to eliminate commodity–money relations. Polish economists who were the spiritual fathers of these reforms shared these views. For example, O. Lange's idea of 'market socialism' of 1956–7 assumed that through trial and error the state is capable of determining prices (as is done by the market). It was also assumed that the market and private property (though small in extent) could also be instruments of central planning.
2. The society: it was assumed that the state knows the objective neeeds of society better than society itself.

The political consequences of the decentralisation reforms were primarily 'limited pluralism' and 'regulation through crisis'.[3] Limited pluralism appeared first in hidden form and then became ever more open in horse-trading among the different bureaucracies: economic, state, party and so on. The bargaining concerned planning targets and the means for their realisation. This resulted in growing anarchy in the system and the actual absence of a central plan. It should be added that it makes no sense to argue over whether the chief ailment of the system was centralisation or anarchy,[4] because these are only two sides of the same coin: the logic of the unitary state, especially at the later stages of its existence.

Since the result of decentralisation is pluralism limited only to the bureaucracy, society has no possibility of realising its interests and values. At the same time, since it is less efficient, the economy is unable to satisfy even the modest material and other needs of the society. The ultimate weapon is social protest, which in order to be effective must be increasingly widespread. The result is a social–political crisis which at first is something exceptional, but which subsequently becomes an integral part of the system as the way in which the power system adapts to the changing needs of society and the economy. The political crisis results in a change of the ruling team, which begins a new political cycle with certain concessions to the rebellious society.

These phenomena are closely interconnected. Limited pluralism leaves the bureaucratic structures untouched because it does not introduce rules of the social and political game on which the society can systematically rely. Between society and the power centre there is no intermediate structure which can guarantee in a form acceptable to everybody the articulation of interests from below and mediation between the various interests and values within society (and between it and the authorities). In short there is no civil society, a sphere in which rules, institutions, agencies, groups, practices and so on allow individuals to seek and satisfy each other's needs. Its emergence would mean not only the separation of state and society but also the existence, as noted above, of an intermediate level, distinct from state and society: public regulatory and welfare bodies, corporate bodies, law courts, political associations, professional organisations, trade unions, self government institutions (local and other) and so on.

The lack of such a structure before 1980 in Poland meant that the rules that existed not only did not ensure greater economic efficiency, but also left the authorities and society in an unresolved conflict. The economic system ran down and the political system (the state) was no longer capable of governing. This accounted for regulation through crisis which, without changing the system as a whole, could only temporarily alleviate such and other problems. This happened in Poland twice: in the period 1956–70 and in the period 1970–80. With hindsight one could say that this was the direct result of the unity of the state and society, while 'civil society depends on their separation',[5] or in other words of the determining role of politics *vis à vis* the economy and society in an authoritarian system, which existed in Poland after 1956 (while before 1956 we had a totalitarian system).

SOCIALISATION REFORM AS A SUBSTITUTE FOR POLITICS

Socialisation means not only moving decisions down to lower levels, but at the same time handing some of these decentralised decisions to the representative bodies of the industrial workforce. A socialisation reform is an attempt not only to make the economy partially autonomous in relation to politics, but also to make society partially autonomous with regard to the economy and politics.

This reform has two sources, economic and social. Its economic sources are linked to the economic crisis which appeared in Poland at the end of the 1970s and once and for all dispelled illusions that attempts to 'improve' the system could be successful. Yet it was qualitatively new social demands and activities, in the form of an emerging civil society, which determined the shape of the proposed reforms. Let us recall that, since the crackdown against striking workers in 1976, Poland had witnessed the emergence of numerous self-organised groups concerned with the defence of their interests, civil rights, social solidarity and so on. Among them were, for example, the Committee for Workers' Defence (KOR), the Society for Academic Courses (the Flying University) and many students' solidarity committees. The best known was the independent, self-governing trade union, Solidarity, which was formed in the summer of 1980. Solidarity was a new mediating institution between the authorities and society. Previously that role had been played, to a degree, by the Catholic Church,[6] but some sociologists were still speaking about a social or institutional vacuum between, on the one hand, the family and small circle of friends and, on the other hand, the nation (and, of course, an alien state).[7]

Emerging institutions had been formed outside the institutional framework of the state. They called themselves independent, self-governing, autonomous, free and so on. This always meant non-regulated by the state. For example, Solidarity was created in opposition to the official trade unions, which were part of the 'transmission belt' structure, which reduced the industrial democracy institutions to passing down decisions from the top to the bottom and not articulating and representing the interests and values of the bottom to the top.

Although new institutions were perceived by the authorities as threats to the state, the leaders of these institutions did not initially call for the abolition of the socialist state. These collective efforts were defined most often as 'an alternative society'. The concept of civil society itself, understood as something separate from the state or in opposition to it, became more popular somewhat later when it was clear that the strategy of 'normalisation' undertaken by the authorities (economic reform being a part of it) was not likely to give the expected results. By the end of the 1980s, people became convinced that the only way to change the situation was to liquidate the existing socialist state, because of its 'unreformability'. What was also new by the end of the 1980s was that the change could not be achieved simply by integrating society around certain noble values such as solidarity, the dignity of man, social autonomy and so on. Those were the main slogans of Solidarity throughout the 1980s. Fortunately society had at its disposal two important resources: the will for a systemic change shared by almost the entire society and various forms of organisation. That is why the idea of alternative society was given another meaning. The emerging civil society was defining itself more and more often as an anti-state; to be more precise, an anti-socialist state.

This sort of understanding of the situation came after a whole decade of searching, which allows us to define the decade as the period of transition. During this period the main vehicles leading to the new era were found in the ideas and practices of socialisation. It was reflected in the following pheonomena:

1.   All attempts to eliminate industrial, social and political conflicts by the authorities were failing. The only way out of the situation was to regulate these conflicts, but this required credible representative institutions. The trade union, Solidarity, became the first body mediating between the monocentric power centre and society.

2.   The incorporation into the political–economic system of independent bodies – trade unions and then employees' councils – took place without changing the political system as a whole. This necessarily produced pressure from industrial workforces and society to make the institutions of industrial democracy substitutes for institutions of political democracy.[8] The authorities were convinced that, as in the past, when they implemented a strategy of normalisation, they would be able to limit these institutions to ceremonial functions. Society, in turn, wanted to use them to effect a qualitative change in the system.

3.   Since the decentralisation reforms were seen as only bureaucratic manoeuvres, it was believed that conflict between the authorities and society could be eliminated by inviting representatives from below to participate in decision-making processes. Hence the

appearance of new actors on the social scene: not only trade union activists and members of employees' councils, but also those from other institutions. Socialisation proceeded under pressure from below, but with the approval of reformist forces within the political establishment. In sum, these moves were more concessions to the rebellious employees than a deliberate implementation of the ideological slogans of self-governing socialism, as in Yugoslavia.

4. An attempt was made by the authorities to transform the bureaucratic-accommodation model into a corporative-negotiatory model. It was a form of concessionary democracy, which meant that the party state elites continued to determine the scope and forms of this democracy.

The question remains as to whether the socialisation reform could have led to the introduction of a qualitatively different political–economic system. One problem rested on the fact that for a long time, particularly in Yugoslavia, the view was widespread that a socialisation reform is 'a third road' between, on the one hand, state socialism with a centrally planned economy, a unitary state (where all legislative, judicial and executive powers are located in one place) and a collectivistic–egalitarian social order and, on the other hand, a private economy, with political pluralism and individual competion. This third road was to be 'a self-governing socialism'.

A good argument can be made for the thesis that socialisation can only be another form of manipulation if the outside system in which the institutions of industrial democracy are located is not changed simultaneously. For example, in Yugoslavia the self-management system really did increase grass-roots participation, but it did not give society influence over the political–economic decisions made at the top. Neither was the economic efficiency of the self-management system impressive,[9] though there is considerable evidence that the self-managed enterprise could be more efficient than the state enterprise, at least in Poland.

In short, a regulated market and concessionary democracy are only instruments in the repertoire of the party state. The thesis of 'a third road' in the form of 'self-managed socialism' so far remains only wishful thinking. Of course the future may bring a more conducive environment for the realisation of the idea.

CIVIL SOCIETY AS A POST-STATE

As I have tried to show, the socialisation paradigm became a transitory compromise formula in conflicts between society and the power centre in the 1980s. This was an outcome of the interaction of many conflicting interests and values, which had to find a practical formula for reconciliation. But we can approach the same problem from another perspective; that is, from that of an ideal which would better suit the parties of the conflict ideologically.

I have already stated that the authorities pursued a sort of neo-corporatist strategy. They tried to co-opt emerging institutions within the existing state structure. Such a strategy is known as state corporatism (another type of corporatism is one constructed from below: societal corporatism). The perfect example of its realisation might be the agreement reached between the authorities and the opposition at the round-table talks; the power centre proposed to the opposition that they compete for 35 per cent of parliamentary seats while the power centre would distribute the remaining seats. One may ask, did Solidarity, as the emanation of civil society, have the ideal of a post-socialist state?

My answer is in the negative, but I would not object to the statement that within Solidarity existed different ideals in relation to the future state. They were certainly not fully formed. Perhaps the best known of them was the idea of a 'self-governing republic'. This seemed to mean a society without a state at all. In a way it resembled the old Marxist idea of the withering away of the state after the completion of the socialist revolution. Let me add that Solidarity rarely invoked socialist writings. But it is a historical fact that Solidarity formally embraced the idea of self-governing republic. The idea was rather vague, but in one area it had a concrete meaning. The Congress held in the autumn of 1981 strongly supported the idea of transforming the state-managed enterprise into a self-managed enterprise. It was a clear option in the direction of participatory democracy, which definitely belongs to the socialist tradition (but not the the tradition of state socialism). At the same time it expressed the idea of a 'post-state'.

When the opposition started to create institutions independent of the state, it had to base the process on state employees, which meant organising them politically. But it was a special type of politics, a type which for some people is not politics at all. The problem is that Solidarity did not seek to take power – which is the essence of any politics. As A.J. Polan writes, Solidarity 'was advancing a concept of politics, that was not about power, but about representation. It rejected the assumption that the articulation of specific interests by particular social groups automatically implied a claim for control of the state'.[10] Solidarity only wanted to represent society. In order to win control over the state, some separation of these two spheres had to be made. In fact Solidarity's depoliticisation strategy represented only one sort of withdrawal from politics – withdrawal from politics, as it was officially defined. As Z. Bauman stresses, Solidarity did not want to enter a dicsourse within the Party's domain, which meant that it would be trapped by the official political game.[11] This happened to be only partly true later when Solidarity leaders, with the approval of society, entered into such a game set up by the Party in 1989 (the round-table talks). One can argue that Solidarity developed a long-range strategy, which proved to be victorious at the end of 1989, but I prefer to treat this victory not as a realisation of the political plan which Solidarity supposedly had (to me it would be a conspiracy theory), but rather as an outcome which came as a combination of planned actions and un- planned opportunities.

Solidarity began to construct a civil society in the workplaces. Initially it organised only those people who were located in the industrial enterprises of large industrial centres. It took the form of a trade union uniting blue-collar workers and professionals. This unity was its characteristic feature. In the past the authorities had been able to separate these two groups. The point I want to make is that Solidarity could not gain lasting control by making one big trade union only. Furthermore the decision to support industrial self-management was not enough. Solidarity had to move to a more political strategy.

A beginning in this direction was made, of course, when Solidarity signed an agreement with the authorities in 1980. It meant that Solidarity could negotiate with them on behalf of society. The agree- ment to form an institution independent from the state was against the philosophy of the system, which claims that it knows the people's interests better than they know them themselves. It was a recognition that it was not discovery of laws of history but conflicting interests in the process of negotiation that could produce the desired outcome.[12] Society was going to be perceived not as one harmonious whole but as a conflict-ridden structure, in which no interest group has permanently established rights. Party–state goals were going to be replaced by procedures as yet unknown. Politicisation of the whole society from above turned out to be 'a negative utopia'.[13] Politics as defined by the unitary state was pathological politics. To some, it meant 'the end of politics' in general, because there was no place for games between various social groups: 'if power has been seized, then the power question in Communist society ceased to be political'.[14]

My point is that the recognition of Solidarity by the authorities saw the beginning of society enjoying its own representation. It automatically meant that the idea of 'end of politics' was itself ended. This simple fact was not recognised by some Solidarity leaders, not only during the 1980s, but even after the formation of a new government by Solidarity. For example, for the people around the former Prime Minister, T. Mazowiecki, the splitting of Solidarity into political parties in 1990 was a dangerous event because, according to their argument, when a party gains state power society loses its defensive capacities. From this perspective, Wałesa's approach was much more realistic. In short, the Solidarity formula was inconsistent. By maintaining unity it was not only preventing internal differentiation and articulation but, as some observed, in a way was helping the socialist state to decide, for example, with whom to negotiate and what should be at stake.[15]

Now the repoliticisation of Solidarity is in full swing. This is so despite the fact that society itself is more interested in economic problems than in political ones (see next section). The problem is that the Solidarity movement gave birth not only to the ideal called the 'self-governing republic', but also to ideals which seem to be far from this idea. The neoliberals who ran the Polish economy in the 1989–91 period were openly against self-management ideas and practices and, knowing their commitment to private property, one might expect that they would oppose trade unions in the future too. They were partly right, because it was practical experience that dispelled illusions concerning the self-managed enterprise. At the same time they seemed to be too fast in drawing conclusions: the fact that a self-managed firm could not work in the state economy should not be surprising, and it does not mean that it could not work in the market economy, though not necessarily as the only model of an enterprise. They were promoting the idea of self-managed economy up to the moment when it became possible to shift from participatory to representative democracy. Industrial democracy institutions were for them only substitutes for politics; that is, measures to undermine the previous system.

Now their ideal is that of Western liberal democracy, with private property, an elitist form of government and the rest. The post-state they want to discuss is the post-socialist state only. They are not against the state in general and only very few of them would be ready to commit themselves to the idea of a self-governing republic (however understood). This idea seems to be more attractive to social democratic forces at the beginning of the 1990s.

CIVIL SOCIETY AS THE PRE-STATE

The rapid collapse of communism in Poland and in other countries caught many people by surprise. This fact may seem surprising in the light of the events and phenomena presented earlier. It has posed two problems: first, the nature of the post-socialist state which Poland needs; second, the ways in which a proper state can be established. Theoretically speaking, it is up to the society to decide what kind of a state would be the best for Poland. To answer that it should be democratic is not precise enough. There are so many democracies, even in the West, that much more has to be agreed in the coming years. The problem is whether the existing civil society is strong enough to produce such a state, especially if one takes into account the conditions of protracted economic crisis, popular expectations for a speedy rise in the standard of living, authoritarian features in the personality of the new president, external uncertainties coming from the region, the civilisational challenges from the external world and so on. All these factors lead many people to question whether the existing civil society is at all capable of achieving a democratic state and a viable market economy.

According to the doctrine of natural law various forms of associations, formed by individuals for the realisation of different interests, must exist before a modern state is born. And the state is then imposed upon them in order 'to regulate them but not to hamper their further development or prevent their continued renewal'.[16] Such a perspective suggests that civil society can also be discussed under the guise of the pre-state.

Such a discussion is going on in Poland at the moment. Economists of a social-democratic orientation speak about the necessity of marketisation. Economists of the neoliberal orientation add that marketisation is not possible without the privatisation programme. Political scientists emphasise the role of political institutions in carrying out such programmes: parliamentary democracy, public opinion, party system, efficient administration, local self-government and so on.[17] Sociologists are worried about the extent of social anomie,[18] and various uncertainties which are brought about not only by the shock therapy of the new government in the economic sphere, but also by the political system, which can either take the form of a paternalistic state or withdraw from its social–economic functions (as is suggested by most of the neoliberals).

Certain conclusions from this debate are clear. First of all, that it will take time to meet the requirements for a mature civil society, a stable political system and viable market economy. Because these goals are far off on the horizon the situation is still fluid; people search for scapegoats and populist tendencies. This increases the propensity to support a strong leader (in the power centre) as well as a readiness to vote for 'a man from nowhere' (a dream which was realised elsewhere): the case of S. Tymiński, who eliminated Prime Minister T. Mazowiecki from the presidential elections of 1990. People dream of 'a normal life' which is not yet available to weary Poles.

One may notice that the process of constructing civil society is even less advanced in some other countries of the region. Y. Afanasyev, the prominent Russian historian, writes about the absence of civil society in the USSR:

> In our amoeba-like social life people are not seen as having different interests or as belonging to different groups. In this society everyone or almost everyone is supposed to be the same; everyone works for the state, everyone is on salary, everyone is on a leash. Most people have not expressed a desire for anything new... Many people continue to have the same old illusions about the great opportunities that may still be open to them under the existing system ... We have a reverse scale of values ... Against the market are almost a majority of all our citizens. For them, the prospect of a market economy resembles a Stalinist exercise in logic: 'I'll force you to be happy, you bastard![19]

In such a situation one should expect, of course, not only evocations of social despair, but also a process of seeking to change reality. This fortunate aspect of the situation is visible in Poland. People propose ways of catching up with history, of learning lessons from the West (though many more are in favour of simply 'imitating it'), debate which ways of acceleration are the most promising and so on. What I would like further to demonstrate is that the process of learning has to be rather slow, and that the outcome is full of uncertainties. To support this opinion I shall present some empirical data from the economic sphere.

MARKETISATION AND PRIVATISATION AS PRECONDITIONS OF A MATURE CIVIL SOCIETY

The 1980s were a decade of searching for democracy. Most of the actions and activities focused on democracy, however defined, though economic crisis directed attention to economic problems. This was so in spite of the efforts of the political centre, which preferred to restrict society's activities to economic reform and leave political reforms untouched. The 1990s, in turn, it is anticipated, will be an economic rather than social or political decade, a decade of searching for a viable form of market economy, though it is obvious that the search for proper political solutions has not ended, as I have tried to show.

The turn taken in thinking and action is also evident in empirical studies of Polish society. They show that economic questions dominate political ones. In the summer of 1989, right after the partially free parliamentary elections, only 27.9 per cent of Poles stated that 'in order to improve the Polish economy one must first give people more democracy'.[20] The majority was of a different opinion: 33.6 per cent stated that 'in order for us to be able to afford to increase democracy we must first overcome the economic crisis' and – in answer to the same question, which means that the answers must be added to the above – 23.3 per cent said that 'the state of our economy does not depend on whether there is democracy or not in our country'.

These findings clearly differ from earlier ones which put politics much higher. The economic questions are most often endorsed by people with lower and middle incomes, women rather than men, older people rather than younger, manual workers rather than professionals, members of the official trade unions rather than members of Solidarity. The percentage differences between these groups are not particularly large (8–15 per cent). Studies which have been made since the one cited also show the same trends: a shift of social attention from politics towards the economy and a higher level of uncertainty about economic problems, especially among the lower-income people and so on.

The rejection of the old command economy which led to the crisis of the system is, of course, universal. The major alternatives to the previous system today are the free market and privatisation. These solutions, however, create a number of dilemmas whose resolution has already begun, but which will last until the economy reaches a state of normality. There are different predictions as to how long this might take. There was no hope within society that this state could be reached overnight, but the hardships of everyday life have led to growing disillusionment. At the time of writing it is only one year since shock therapy was introduced in Poland, at the beginning of 1990. the new government adopted an economic programme of neoliberal orientation, sponsored by the International Monetary Fund (IMF) and other international economic and political agencies. The programme is still being realised despite dissatisfaction in Polish society. It has already led to the defeat of the government which introduced it. It has already led to the formation of splinter groups within Solidarity, especially a 'Solidarity of Labour', which opposes the programme from a social–democratic platform.[21]

I mention these empirical observations because they confirm a certain ambivalence which had already existed when the 1989 study was carried out. The results of the study showed an almost universal endorsement of the models of a Western private market economy, but simultaneously the widespread acceptance of many solutions from the state economy. I shall give some empirical evidence for this thesis.

We put the question: 'There are many ideas and suggestions for solving the economic and social crisis in our country. We have listed some of them below. Do you agree or disagree with each of these suggestions?' Respondents had the possibility of accepting or rejecting various methods taken from Western economies. All of them were accepted, though the degree of acceptance differed from question to question (answers in percentages):

- inefficient workers should be fired   88.8
- incomes should be strongly differentiated depending on qualification and efficiency   85.6
- free competition between companies, like that in the West is
  approved   81.2
- full freedom for the private sector should be ensured   73.0
- state-owned property should be leased to private persons   64.6
- the Polish market should be totally open to investment from the
  West   62.6
- the risk of unemployment should be accepted   46.6

On the other hand, there is widespread acceptance of the interventionist role of the state in economic and social areas. Listed below are the percentages of those who agreed with the opinion that the state should be concerned with the following problems and solutions:

- ensuring work for all wanting to work   90.2
- controlling prices   87.8
- controlling profits of state companies   83.6
- compensating for price increases   81.7
- controlling profits of private enterprises   72.3
- making decisions about liquidation or creation of new firms 71.9
- reducing differences in incomes between rich and poor   68.3
- establishing areas in the economy in which private companies can be formed   67.5
- helping companies with production or economic difficulties 52.2

These findings show an extremely high degree of acceptance of the methods of the market economy. The exception was unemployment, but even here the percentage of acceptance exceeds the percentage of rejection (46.6 and 34.6 respectively). This may be evidence of unfamiliarity with the real nature of unemployment, which Polish society had not faced before 1989. It may also show that Poland is almost desperately ready to opt for a vision which at least promises to run the economy according to different rules. The result is even more impressive if we notice that supporters of market economy methods constitute a majority of society, in particular those better educated, with higher wages, men, specialists of various sorts, urban residents, those who work on their own account, managers, members of the Party as well as members of Solidarity. One may therefore speak of the mythologisation of the benefits of a market economy and even of a utopian view of the market economy. A fascination with the successes of the Western economy certainly does not go hand-in-hand with awareness of its rules. That is why the introduction of the market economy seems as easy as buying a gadget in a supermarket. Such attitudes suggest that prospects for the imitation of the West are great, which seems to me a rather naive opinion.

The findings also show a widespread acceptance of the interventionist role of the state, not only in social, but also in economic areas. They allow us to identify a considerable lack of cohesion in society, which is ready to choose conflicting methods from economies with different logic. Of course, these different types of logic can be partially reconciled within the conception of a social market economy or, even better, the welfare state. This would mean recognising the market as a general regulator in economic mechanisms and also recognising the state as a supplementary corrective mechanism when there are social reasons to do so. Though solutions of this kind have been practised in the Western world, in Poland they are still only rather vague slogans and, what is more, are often criticised by neoliberals as methods which are not affordable by Poland at the moment. The reality is, however, that the state was and still is considered as an actor, not only on the political, but also on the economic scene. Striking employees, for example, address their demands in 1991 – for the ending of the state-imposed tax on excessive wage-increases – to the government rather than to the factory managers, exactly as they did a few years earlier. As before the state is still perceived as the main author of economic changes (and not the enterprises themselves).[22]

Marketisation now goes together with privatisation in all discussions. The problem of changes in property rights is most often reduced to the question of private ownership. In fact there is widespread approval in society of private property, while at the same time there is not much for state ownership, though it embraces 80 per cent of the economy. Our study shows that private ownership is seen as a desirable form by 68.8 per cent and as a dominant form by 26.4 per cent. Among its supporters are: much more frequently men than women, the youngest and oldest age groups, the self-employed, those with higher wages, much more rarely members of the Party and official trade unions (membership of Solidarity had no significant influence).

The problem is that society does not see the question of ownership as a clear-cut choice between private and state ownership, but seems to accept the principles of a multisectoral economy in which there would also be a place for the co-operative sector, communal property and the property of employees' self-management bodies. Various forms of social ownership are supported by 46.8 per cent of society, but as the dominant form in the future only by 16.3 per cent, which is half as many as private ownership. Finally every fifth respondent regards state ownership as a desirable form of ownership but only 6.4 per cent are willing to accept it as the dominant form in the future. Thus doctrinal positions evident in Poland now are in conflict with the social vision of changes in property rights, a more adequate concept than the privatisation propagated by the neoliberals.

Other dilemmas concern the scope and pace of creating a free market and property changes. The way these dilemmas are solved will determine the depth of transformation and the identity of the system. For many people of a liberal orientation the liquidation of private ownership was a necessary condition for the monopolisation of power in the previous system. For example, A.Z.Kaminski writes that state ownership became a condition of the dictatorship of the revolutionary avant-garde.[23] No doubt this is how it was in the communist system, though there are also other arrangements that give a similar result: the Nazi system in Germany was created under the conditions of a private economy. The real question is whether the creation of a free market with privatisation is the best road to a better future.

Looking at this historically, one can say that the private market economy is only one of the paths to modernisation, though it is the road that has brought most success in the West. Even if Poland wants to follow the same path, this does not mean that the success of the West will be repeated because the economic, social, political and, most of all, historical circumstances such as existed there might not be repeated in Poland. The rush to capitalism, then, should be viewed as ideologically biased, as J.K. Galbraith noted: 'What is offered is an ideological construct that exists all but entirely in the minds and notably in the hopes of the donor. It bears no relation to reality: it is what I have elsewhere called primitive ideology.'[24] Doubts arise, then, not so much in connection with the Western model itself although one should, of course, be aware of its negative sides too) but with respect to the possibilities of its imitation. Exact imitation seems to me impossible, as it was impossible to transplant elements of the Western system in the past. I have in mind 'a third road', one understood as a mixture or convergence of two different systems as predicted in past decades by many theoreticians and practitioners.

The debate is heavily imbued with ideology. Let me add that, while the triumphant neoliberals are ready to imitate the West, they simultaneously reject another type of reality which is also present in the West in the form of social–democratic patterns. What people from the East admire in the West is not actually capitalism, Galbraith also quite rightly noted, but a still imperfect social democracy.[25] Why then should we in Poland introduce something which already belongs to the past in many countries of the West? Instead, why not try to utilise experiences which are closer to people's expectations; for example, as I have tried to demonstrate, a mixture of market and the welfare state. I am of the opinion that the debate could be more fruitful if Poles accepting Western experience would try realistically to search for so-called 'organic development', an approach which combines our various assets with ideas and practices coming from a challenging world.[26] The problem is whether Polish society is able to reach that kind of understanding of the situation. It leads me to pose a final question: what is the nature of the linkages between economics, politics and society?

CONCLUSION: IS THERE A WAY OUT OF THE VICIOUS CIRCLE?

The mechanisms of social–economic development in socialist countries have been described and explained on the basis of simple, single-factor models. The political factor was singled out first. It was assumed that the political bureaucracy embodies a new type of power which can determine what happens in the economic or social system. In many of the theories formulated in the West, as well as in the East, the role of society was clearly underestimated and the role of politics over-estimated.

In the 1960s and 1970s, again one-sidedly, the role of main driving force in social and political development was ascribed either to economic growth (in the West) or to scientific–technological revolution (in the East). The next one-sidedness appeared in the 1980s, when mass social protest in Poland led to the creation of Solidarity, which helped the formulation of a new set of theories, in which society or the civil society is seen as the demiurge of change – including that in the political and economic spheres.

I claim that, irrespective of the historical adequacy of some of these models,[27] which was sometimes greater, sometimes lesser (for example, the totalitarian state theory was adequate for the Soviet Union during 1930–50, but no longer for Poland after 1956), they are even less adequate today, when post-socialist countries are in severe crisis, while analysis of Poland in the 1980s casts doubt on their being useful at all. The problem lies rather in the point of contact of these systems than in treating them in isolation.

As I have tried to show, the interconnections between politics, economics and society were negative in Poland throughout the 1980s. I call this 'a vicious circle'. Neither the decentralisation reform before 1980 nor the socialisation reform after 1980 had any chance of success because of this. The point of contact between the three component systems is for me the starting-point in the search for ways to improve the situation. All these domains are equally important. If the matter is formulated differently illusions are only multiplied. For example, there is the belief that economic reform could be carried out easily if the political leadership really wanted it. The alternative to single-factor models becomes multi-factor ones. The solution suggested is a trans-formation of negative linkages into positive ones. Theoretically speaking, this is feasible: all of these system are now recognised but, as I have noted, progress towards real change is still considered inadequate to expectations.

The main question seems to be the cohesiveness of these three system. Neoliberals make a good case in emphasising the need for the autonomy of these systems in relation to each other.[28] Depoliticisation of the economy from above seems to be as important for them as depoliticisation from below. That is why in Poland they are against the socialisation paradigm (against employees' councils, even against trade unions and so on), even if they are of Solidarity origin. Social democrats, in turn, argue that, under conditions of crisis, the strategy of neoliberals threatens the basic standard of living, which is a plausible argument after the shock therapy used by the new government. In their opinion it is impossible to abandon active government intervention, not only in distribution (social policy) but also in economic policy. In short they stress the necessity for correlation between these two systems. These two options have their populist offshoots, which accentuate either the legitimate claims of society or the necessity to speed up privatisation.

Both sides have good arguments. Excessive dependency by society upon the political system would damage its aspirations. If society were emancipated for diverse forms of involvement in state affairs. Participatory bodies are now being rejected and in their place representative democracy institutions are favoured. Moves towards the autonomy of society are thus impeded. We can speak only of the relative autonomy of society.

This also means that the political system should not be autonomous *vis à vis* society. Obviously, similar arguements can be presented in relation to economic change. Regardless of the efforts of neoliberals to depoliticise the economy the government is still the main author of changes in the economic sphere, and it is expected to continue to be so in the near future. Hence again a more proper concept is that of relative autonomy rather than full autonomy. One could say that the crux of the matter is to find the right mix, which requires real professional knowledge in the unusual circumstances which exist nowadays in Poland and in the other countries of the region.

All of these considerations lead me to believe that we do not yet know what is the destination. It is still premature to predict what will emerge in Poland. I am not alone in voicing such an opinion. R. Dahrendorf has said: 'I do not believe in "a change of the system". In fact, I believe that we are witnessing a departure from the notion of "change of the system" towards a more open concept, which does not mean either retaining the old system or replacing socialism with capitalism'.[29] This sounds good, but it lacks a sense of direction and purpose, which are so important in social activities. Discussion of economic change and civil society does not lead to any definite conclusion. Exact profiles of coming developments are unknown. I have tried to show how economic and social, and also political dilemmas, make this so. Simultaneously I have enumerated certain conditions of success that are hard to meet. For the first time since 1945, however, there appears to be a real chance of meeting them. This attempt is fully supported by Polish society, now in the stage of transforming itself into a mature civil society. To reach a stage of maturity becomes possible, however, only when economic changes make marketisation and property changes effective. The state can help to make such a change slower or faster. All the above factors justify talking about qualitative changes not only *in* the system but *to* the system as such, although its shape cannot be described in precise terms as yet.

A prominent American economist aptly noted that one really has to work hard for development not to go forward.[30] If this is true, then one must be convinced that at least some successes await the Poles, because there is no doubt that their society not only suffers greatly but also tries hard to make its future better.

Notes

1. The distinction between civil society understood as the pre-state, the anti-state and the post-state has been taken from N. Bobbio, *Democracy and Dictatorship* (Cambridge: Polity, 1989). See also Z. A. Pelczynski (ed.), *The State and Civil Society* (Cambridge: Cambridge University Press, 1984) and A. Sales, 'The private, the public and civil society: social realms and power structures', paper presented at the conference on 'The World in Transition', Pułtusk (Poland) June 1990.
2. See W. Brus, 'Evolution of the communist economic system: scope and limits', in V. Nee and D. Stark (eds), *Remaking the Economic Institutions of Socialism: China and Eastern Europe* (Stanford: Stanford University Press, 1989).
3. See W. Morawski, 'Politics', in 'Three types of economic reforms in Poland', *Polish Sociological Bulletin*, No. 1, 1989.
4. See P. Bożyk, *Marzenia i rzeczywistość* (Dreams and Reality) (Warsaw: PIW, 1989).
5. See M. D. Kennedy, *Professionals, Power and Solidarity in Poland* (Cambridge: Cambridge University Press, 1991).
6. See B. Szajkowski, 'The Catholic Church in defense of civil society in Poland', in B. Misztal (ed.), *Poland after Solidarity* (New Brunswick and

Oxford: Transaction Books, 1985).

7. See S. Nowak, 'Społeczeństwo polskie czasu kryzysu w swietle teorii anomii' (Polish society at a time of crisis in the light of the theory of anomie), in *Polska 2000* (Poland 2000) (Wrocław: Ossolineum, 1984).

8. See W. Morawski, 'Self-management and economic reform', in J. Koralewicz *et al.* (eds), *Crisis and Transition. Polish Society in the 1990s* (Oxford: Berg, 1987).

9. H. Lydall, *Yugoslavia in Crisis* (Oxford: Clarendon Press, 1989).

10. See A. J. Polan, *Lenin and the End of Politics* (London: Methuen, 1984) p. 3.

11. See Z. Bauman, 'On the maturation of socialism', *Telos* No. 47 (Spring 1981).

12. See C. E. Lindblom, *Politics and Markets* (New York: Basic Books, 1977). See also V. Ostrom, *The Intellectual Crisis in American Public Administration*, 2nd edn (Tuscaloosa and London: University of Alabama Press, 1989).

13. See A. Arato and M. Vajda, 'The limits of the Leninist opposition', *New German Critique*, No. 19 (Winter 1980).

14. See A. Zinoviev, *The Reality of Communism* (London: Gollancz, 1984) p. 194.

15. See J. Staniszkis, 'Self-limiting revolution', *Sisyphus*, No. 3 (1982). See also M. Markus, 'Constitution and functioning of a civil society in Poland', in Misztal (ed.), *Poland after Solidarity*.

16. See Bobbio, *Democracy and Dictatorship*, p. 24.

17. See W. Lamentowicz, 'Polska droga do demokracji' (Polish road to democracy), in *Głowne problemy dzisiejszej i przyszkW370ej Rzeczpospolitej* (Main Problems of the Present and Future Republic) (Warsaw: Warsaw University, 1990).

18. See M. Marody, *'Dylematy postaw politycznych i orientacji świato-poglądowy'* (Dilemmas of Political Attitudes and Worldview Orientations) (mimeo, Warsaw: Institute of Sociology, 1990).

19. See Y. Afanasyev, 'The coming dictatorship', *New York Review of Books*, 31 January 1991.

20. Empirical studies conducted by B. Cichomski and W. Morawski, Institute of Sociology, Warsaw University: 'Are we living in a just society?' and 'The plan and market *vis à vis* the social structure' (1986–90).

21. See J. Poprzeczko, 'Przeciw utopii liberalnej' (Against the liberal utopia), *Polityka*, 9 February 1991.

22. See L. Kolarska-Bobińska, 'The Changing Face of Civil Society in Eastern Europe, mimeo, Institute of Philosophy and Sociology, Polish Academy of Sciences, Warsaw, 1990.

23. See A. Z. Kamiński, 'Reformability and development potential of political economic regimes', paper presented in Dubrovnik, April 1990, in the course on 'Economic Sociology in Comparative Perspective'.

24. See J. K. Galbraith, 'The rush to capitalism', *New York Review of Books*, 25 October 1990.

25. Ibid.

26. See J. Kornai, *The Road to a Free Economy* (New York and London: Norton, 1990).

27. See T. Jones, 'Models of socialist development', *International Journal of Comparative Sociology*, Vol. 24 (January–April 1983).
28. See F. A. Hayek, *New Studies in Philosophy, Politics and the History of Ideas* (Chicago: University of Chicago Press, 1978).
29. 'Pułapki demokracji' (The pitfalls of democracy), a statement by R. Dahrendorf for *Trybuna*, 8 March 1990.
30. See M. Olson, *The Rise and Decline of Nations* (New Haven and London: Yale University Press, 1982).

6 Dilemmas and Controversies Concerning Leadership Recruitment in Eastern Europe

Jacek Wasilewski

INTRODUCTION

Eastern Europe is currently undergoing a phase of transition. This is possibly the only statement concerning the area upon which all researchers would readily agree. The issue of *transition from what* and, even more, *to what*, is a moot point. It is most commonly pointed out that these changes signify a transition from communist dictatorship to democracy. However the experiences of respective countries are quite diverse and in some cases serious doubts as to whether the changes will lead to democracy could be substantiated.

This issue, although vital for the assessement and prediction of the development of the situation in Eastern Europe, is not the purpose of this chapter. Considering that we experienced profound systemic changes (although we are not always able to state definitely what their outcome will be) we shall deal only with one particular aspect of those changes, namely leadership recruitment. This process seems to be of particular importance in the realisation of new socioeconomic programmes, and consequently to the success or failure of the reforms started in all countries of the region. At the same time it is a process which evokes popular interest and emotion, often leading to conflict. Such emotion and conflict can be observed on a daily basis in all countries of the former Soviet bloc.

NOMENKLATURA PATTERNS OF ELITE RECRUITMENT

In communist Poland, and similarly in other East European countries, the process of leadership recruitment followed three basic paradigms. First, the *communist–combatant* model appears to have been in practice towards the end of the Second World War and in the years immediately after it. At that time the key criteria for leadership selection were: (1) loyalty to the contemporary communist principles confirmed by membership of the Polish Communist Party and, after it was dissolved by Stalin in 1938, of the Polish Workers' Party; and/or (2) active participation in the political organisations which functioned in the Soviet Union in the 1940s, later in Poland; and/or (3) a letter of recommendation from the time of military service in the Polish Army formed initally in 1943 in the Soviet Union.

Second, the *communist–combatant–prolaterian* model was established in the Stalinist period. On the one hand it tightened the selection criteria used in the first model, but, on the other, owing to the greater number of posts to be filled, it included people of the 'proper' stock and class membership in the privileged group. People of either urban or rural proletarian origin supporting the new regime had a good chance of direct promotion to important posts.

Third, the *party specialist* model was introduced after October 1956. The changes in selection criteria introduced at this time were to include both political and meritocratic requirements. In order to satisfy the former, a candidate was expected to be a member of the communist party (or its political satellites), while for the latter he was to hold a college diploma. In practice, however, the candidate's merit was subordinate to his or her political qualifications. Furthermore occupational credentials were often considered a pure formality.

At the base of all three models lay the system of *nomenklatura*. The term '*nomenklatura*' is used in three ways. First, it is a mechanism of selection and recruitment of personnel: candidates are either proposed and nominated or at least endorsed by the proper body of party organisation. Second, it refers to a list of posts which are subject to this mechanism. Third, the *nomenklatura* are a group of people who were appointed to these posts according to the aforementioned mechanism.

The positions available exclusively to party nominees covered all spheres of social, political and economic life. Thus a *nomenklatura* system of personnel recruitment became one of the means of exercising totalitarian control over society. In addition it should be noted that the principle of *nomenklatura* was an essential characteristic of the communist political system. It was by no means simply evidence of its abnormality or pathology. Instead, any deviation from the *nomenklatura* system was considered pathological. The history of the communist movement is littered with victims charged with such deviation. It would be extremely difficult to find an equivalent discriminating mechanism inherent in contemporary societies' political systems (with the exception of South African apartheid). Obviously in many societies discrimination, including political discrimination, does exist, but it is not essential to system maintenance. The principle of *nomenklatura* was essential to the maintenance of neo-Stalinism.

Moreover the term '*nomenklatura*' is linked with the entire set of pejorative societal impressions, assessments and stereotypes. These mainly pertain to *nomenklatura*'s qualifications, privileges, and way of wielding power.

The professional qualifications of *nomenklatura* are perceived as being insufficient and their managerial experience lacking, while their skills in the field of manipulations and intrigues are very well developed. The latter skills are usually associated with considerable involvement of *nomenklatura* in informal structures, coteries and client–patron relationships. *Nomenklatura's* political vulnerability is of great importance. In the system which is characterised by instability and inconsistency of goals, this vulnerability leads to frequent changes of personnel and the breaking of the personality and morale of individuals.

Societal perception of *nomenklatura* material and non-material privileges is entirely negative. This strong disapproval springs from the following facts:

- goods in a society are distributed according to two separate mechanisms, one utilised for *nomenklatura*, the other for the rest of society;
- the mechanism utilised for *nomenklatura* is based on the political usefulness of individuals at a given moment, and has nothing to do with their contribution to the national product;
- *nomenklatura*'s share in goods distribution is disproportionately high compared to that of other social groups.

Altogether privileges of *nomenklatura* are seen as totally unjustified and are treated as evidence of the exploitation of society.

The three models described above reflect the development of recruitment patterns and are highly characteristic of post-revolutionary regimes. Immediately after a successful revolution, maintaining orthodoxy of revolutionary ideology was essential, as was the involvement of those who were established participants in the revolutionary movement. However it soon became apparent that the practical tasks of governing required other skills and qualifications as well. Hence, at this juncture, there appeared the fundamental contradiction between ideological loyalty and strictly technical and managerial expertise. The attempt at solving the problem (known in the literature as the 'reds versus experts' cleavage) led to the pattern of a *party specialist*; that is, promotion into leadership posts only of '*our*' (that is, *red*) experts. In the 1980s, mainly owing to Solidarity, the communist regime in Poland was no longer able to ignore the popular demand for meritocratic selection of the elite. At this time a new pattern of recruitment was introduced. It was to be based on meritocratic credentials: the political activity or membership of candidates was supposed to be of no practical relevance. However the nominees were required to observe the constitutional principles of the political system, and thus the model of a *loyal expert* became the first attempt to meet, at least halfway, social expectations of a departure from the principle of *nomenklatura*. At the same time it allowed for the elimination of political dissidents and opponents of the redistributive economic system from the *pool of eligibles*. The observance of constitutional principles involved recognition of the leadership of the communist party, acceptance of 'brotherly co-operation' with the Soviet Union and the existence of a centrally-planned and state-owned economy.

The model of a loyal expert has never been fully put into practice. It has remained a theoretical formula which served exclusively propagandist purposes. In the 1980s the *nomenklatura* proved to be strong enough to control the recruitment processes to its own ranks.

LEADERSHIP RECRUITMENT DILEMMAS IN POST-COMMUNIST EASTERN EUROPE

At the time of writing, in the middle of 1990, the issue of leadership recruitment in Eastern Europe looks different in those countries which have had some experience of institutionalised opposition to the communist regime, and therefore where the process of change is much more advanced, from those where the process is in its preliminary stages.

In Romania and Bulgaria, where organisations independent of the control of the single-party order did not exist at all or operated to a very limited degree, the recruitment of both political elite (top power elite) and new bureaucratic apparatus must take place, *nolens volens*, from the ranks of the former *nomenklatura*. The best opportunities seem to be available to those who, either because of membership of the 'wrong' political faction of of personally being in the 'bad books' of the boss, were, in the past, removed from the exercise of power. The problem these societies face is that they must create a completely new political elite and the crux seems to be that, to a great degree, the process must be undertaken by the people of the old elite.

The situation is quite different in Poland and Hungary. In communist Poland there has always existed an institution independent of party influence, namely the Catholic Church. Its constancy and moral authority constituted significant factors in the overall attitude of the society. The very fact of the Church's presence had some influence on the existence of Poland of institutionalised groups opposing the communist regime.

Since the mid-1960s the crystallisation of *political society* in Poland has been accelerating. Peoples' activities outside the Party/state structures and independent institutions have been broadening steadily, to the point where, in the late 1970s, they affected nearly all spheres of human life. The phenomenon of Solidarity, a legal, large-scale national organisation with a fully-developed formal structure at all levels, would not have been possible without such experience. Thus the birth of Solidarity was a rebirth of *civil society* in Poland. Martial law temporarily weakened but by no means put to an end the institutional activity of Solidarity, or to the other independent political groups. Civil society was forced into a period of dormancy through the martial law years, but only to become more vigorous than ever in 1989.

Independent organisations in Poland, to a slightly lesser degree in Hungary and partially also in Czechoslovakia, managed to create a political counter-elite which is numerous (at least in Poland) and experienced enough to assume the leading role in the transitional period. However these organisations have not been able to develop their own bureaucratic apparatus, a whole mass of officials who could now take over thousands of positions in the state and economic administration, in local governments and in self-governing bodies. Such an idea did not lie at the foundation of those independent organisations, whose methods tended on principle to avoid formalism and bureaucracy, ever-present in 'real socialism'. Hence qualified and experienced administrators not 'infected' with communist pragmatism and independent of the previous political and personal coteries simply do not exist, and this applies to all three countries mentioned above.

The problem to be solved by the societies of these countries, and by Polish society in particular, does not then consist of creating a new national political elite, unlike, for example, the situation of Romania. For such an elite has been spontaneously created in the course of the struggle against the communist dictatorship. Today we face a new situation which requires 'normal' and stable means of leadership recruitment and – most probably – also a new type of leader: a leader for a time of peace, not war. There exist, therefore, two groups of questions to which the young democracies of East Central Europe must find answers: (1) Should the old bureaucracy be totally abandoned and replaced by the new one, or, rather, should the former remain and be turned into a competent administrative apparatus loyal to the new leadership? (2) In what way and on the basis of what criteria should the elite formed at the time of struggle for democracy be renewed? Ought the recruitment of the new elite be open to all social *milieux* and movements? Or should it rather be limited to those political groups which were instrumental in overthrowing the system of 'real social-ism'? If it is to be open, should it then be accessible to the former communist establishment? If it is to be limited to the powers opposing the communist regime, should all of them be guaranteed participation in the new elite? Ought this privilege to be granted also to those of extreme radical opinions? Should it be a limited recruitment and, if so, does it stand in agreement with democratic ideals and equal chances for all? If recruitment is limited, will it not lead to new *nomenklatura*?

All these questions have obviously been applicable for centuries and have invariably been posed at the time of radical political changes. Nevertheless, on every single occasion, they must be answered anew. The answers given in the past might be helpful, but the current situation demands answers of its own.

Both dilemmas, that concerning the bureaucratic apparatus and that connected with the recruitment of the top political elite, are sources of social controversies and are proving to be the subject-matter of debate and political struggle.

CONTROVERSIES CONCERNING THE BUREAUCRATIC APPARATUS: DOES THE OLD NOMENKLATURA STILL RULE?

The issue of the bureaucratic apparatus in Poland seems to be approached in three basic ways. (1) The government opts for a prudent personnel policy, employing the qualifications and experience of the old bureaucracy for the needs of the new system. The argument given for this approach is that the highest officials of the former adminis-tration have already been discussed or will be in the near future. (The process is time-consuming as each case must be considered individually, with scrupulous observance of law and respect paid to human dignity.) It is said that competent officials of middle-rank and low positions should be allowed to remain, mainly because we do not have at our disposal experienced administrative personnel and the number of new candidates not associated with the former system is far from sufficient.

Hence, for the proponents of this alternative, the main issue associated with state personnel policy is not at all the question as to whether the old administrative stratum should be dismissed but rather how to change it into an efficient bureaucratic apparatus loyal to the new government. Proponents justify this attitude with both pragmatic and moral reasons. The government's standpoint is shared, for obvious reasons, by old administrative personnel still employed in various governmental agencies.

(2) The intermediate stand, represented by the moderate circles within Solidarity, many activists of the Citizens' Committee and part of the public, recognises some of the government's reasons but it demands a radical speeding-up of the process of personnel change and is of the opinion that this change should affect a much greater number of officials.

(3) The contrary attitude to the governmental one is represented by a large part of the public, new parties and political groups (of centrist and rightist programmes) as well as the radical wing of Solidarity. The proponents of this stand think that all administrative personnel should be vetted (this applies also to officials outside the state administration) and they propose a general 'purge' of the administrative structures. They insist that all officials associated with the previous regime be debarred from any influence on public matters, even at the lowest level.

The followers of this alternative, which seems to be favoured by a large part of society (perhaps even the majority), think that the old *nomenklatura* in Poland has not yet been abolished. They claim that, generally speaking, the very same people still hold the same (or equivalent) positions. In this case *nomenklatura* is defined very broadly as the group that embodies all people holding higher and middle-rank posts in various bureaucratic structures, and some even include in this term all those implementing policy.

In such an extreme form, these assessments are far from accurate. One should, however, keep in mind that public opinion is to a considerable degree shaped by individual cases, especially if they are sufficiently high-profile. Hence the opinion held by the public is largely influenced by the presence of a few former party *apparatchiks* still holding important posts. How the fate of the former *nomenklatura* is generally perceived is also relevant here.

The dominant opinion in Polish society seems to be that both the members of the previous power elite as well as officials of the administrative apparatus, and people connected with it, managed to secure privileged positions in the new economic and political system. These placements have been secured in two basic ways. The former *nomenklatura* have either retained their previous positions or they have managed to transform their privileged positions within the power structure into privileged positions in the economic sphere. The latter phenomenon, known in Poland under the term of *affranchisement of the nomenklatura*, consists of the former power elite making a shift to the private or semi-private business domain. Making use of their formal position and favourable placement in informal political and economic networks, and taking full advantage of the first market-oriented economic reforms, these *apparatchiks* succeed in establishing various companies which feed on state resources (energy, machinery, raw materials, manpower, business networks) to make private profit. Another way of transforming *political capital* into *market capital* is the occupation of strategic posts in private business by former *nomenklatura* people (particularly in Polish–foreign joint ventures).

It must be stated here that the public opinion of the former *nomenklatura* is to a great extent justified. It must be added, however, that many of them retired, some went back to their previous occupations and a considerable number who remained within the power apparatus were shifted to lower (non-*nomenklatura*) posts.

All in all, the controversies and dilemmas related to the administrative apparatus are in most cases well-grounded and arguments supporting the different options are meaningful.

CURRENT PATTERNS OF LEADERSHIP RECRUITMENT: DO WE HAVE A NEW NOMENKLATURA?

Equally controversial is the problem of new leadership recruitment. The government has declared a system of open and meritocratic selection of personnel. However it did not fail to mention that loyalty to the new authorities should be an important criterion of that recruitment. In other words, a variant of the *loyal expert* model has been proclaimed.

Critics of the new government, initially those close to the former regime, but now also those related in some way to Solidarity, maintain that the old *nomenklatura* has been to a considerable degree replaced by the new one. They claim that the current system of recruitment is basically not unlike the old one; that is, to a large measure determined by political factors and thus limited to the followers of a given political strategy.

For nearly a year now – claim the critics – the new authorities have made use of recruitment models practically equivalent to those employed by communists. They form nearly exact counterparts to the three *nomenklatura* models mentioned above. First, there is the *dissident–combatant* model. Virtually all leaders and advisors of Solidarity and of the movements associated with Solidarity in the 1980s occupy strategic posts within the new power structure (in the Parliament, government, economy, mass media, and so on). This perfectly matches the principle mentioned earlier, that, after a victorious revolution, early involvement in the movement is an important recruitment criterion.

Second, the *dissident–combatant–'non-regime'* model: when Solidarity and opposition leaders in general took over top posts in the power structure, it soon appeared that the number of positions to be filled was greater than the number of available *dissidents–combatants*. Hence in the *pool of eligibles* were included people who had not been particularly active in the fight against the communist dictatorship but at the same time had not been directly involved in the former structures, or who, in good time, had changed their attitudes to appropriate ones. Many of these originate in Catholic and independent intellectual *milieux*.

Third, the *Solidarity–specialist* model: this pattern of recruitment has not been employed too frequently; nevertheless there have been instances of some positions being made available only to members of Solidarity, of a recommendation from the local branches of the union being a necessary condition for a candidate, and of various Solidarity bodies endorsing or refusing to endorse a candidate.

Thus claims of a *new nomenklatura* exist in conjunction with complaints that the old system continues. These points are not necessarily contradictory, as it will have happened that some members of the old *nomenklatura* still maintain their power, whereas newcomers to the power apparatus are chosen according to new rules, but ones which are equivalent to the principles of *nomenklatura*.

Are critics of the current policy of recruitment essentially right? Do we actually face a new *nomenklatura*, a new political monopoly, and a new single party? These general questions call for more than simple 'yes' or 'no' answers. The fact that the new political elite is recruited from the victorious political side is a natural outcome of radical systemic change. Hence it does not provide sufficient evidence for the existence of that very specific political phenomenon we call *nomenklatura*.

PARLIAMENTARY REPRESENTATION OF SOLIDARITY

The assessment of the current patterns of recruitment of the political and bureaucratic elite calls for more than just quoting superficial data and citing incidental impressions (particularly when strongly determined by political preferences). It requires reliable data on the professional and political careers of new leaders, their education, attitudes and system of values. Today such data do not exist, hence there can be no reliable answers. However it does not necessarily follow that the personnel policies currently followed should not be evaluated at all and that one should refrain from voicing doubts or objections to their general direction.

There is no doubt that taking power away from the communists has radically changed the social base from which the elite is recruited, enlarging it by including those *milieux* which used to be on the margin of public life. In the recently published collection of biographies of MPs and senators elected from the Solidarity list of nominees in June 1989,[3] one can find information supporting this statement. The booklet contains short CVs of 161 MPs and 99 senators who were elected to the National Assembly in the elections, the formula of which had been agreed upon at the Round-Table debates (65 per cent of seats in the Parliament reserved for the communist coalition and contested elections to the Senate). Obviously data concerning legislators cannot be used as the basis of far-reaching generalisations – it is a specific group formed in very specific circumstances. Nevertheless it seems to illustrate reasonably well the new trends in leadership recruitment.

When analysing the social backgrounds of MPs and senators we do not observe any particularly striking differences in comparison to the origin of various *nomenklatura* bodies. Out of 260 people, 16 per cent were brought up in blue-collar workers' families, 26 per cent in peasant families, and 46 per cent in white-collar ones. What is interesting, however, is that already, at the level of social origin, the social base seems to have been broadened: nearly 8 per cent of parliamentary representatives of Solidarity come either from big land-owning families

(4.6 per cent) or the bourgeoisie (3.1 per cent); that is, the categories formerly totally eliminated by communists from official political activity.

As many as 38 per cent of Solidarity legislators mention in their CVs family traditions of freedom, patriotic or anti-communist struggle, usually connected with the fight for independence in the years 1916–21 (Piłsudski's Legions, Polish–Soviet war of 1920) or with the Second World War and the period immediately after it (Home Army, deportations to the heartland of Russia and so on). This shows clearly that family tradition had an important impact on the bringing-up of subsequent generations. At the same time it proves that standard sociological data on social origin defined by parents' occupations are not able to shed any light on the different modes of the socialisation of future Solidarity representatives in legislators bodies.

Occupational *milieux* in which Solidarity legislators pursued their professional careers at first sight do not differentiate them, by any considerable degree, from the representatives of previous elites. But also in this case it is important not to mistake the superficial similarity of occupational titles. The careers of two men of the same profession, one of whom was a member of the communist party and the other of the oppositional organisation, would be diametrically opposed.

Another obvious difference in occupational structure between the old elite and Solidarity legislators is the lack of any party *apparatchiks* in the new elite. It should also be noted that there exists a group (4.2 per cent) whose professional career is virtually impossible to define, for either it has not fully started yet (students) or it has been so complicated as a result of repression and political difficulty that it could best be characterised in the following way: 'profession: political prisoner'. However a great majority have identifiable professional careers which in some cases show a surprising lack of continuity (dramatic change of workplace or occupation owing to political repression).

The greates number of Solidarity legislators come from intellectual and intelligentsia circles and they constitute over 70 per cent of the total (scientists and scholars, 19.2 per cent; lawyers, 9.6 per cent; teachers, 8.1 per cent; journalists, editors, writers and so on, 8.1 per cent; economists and related occupations, 5 per cent; physicians, 4.2 per cent, engineers and technocrats, 15.8 per cent; representatives of other 'intelligentsia' professions, 3.9 per cent). It is quite striking that only one representative is a clerk. Workers constitute 7.7 per cent and farmers 12.7 per cent.

It seems almost redundant to say that the experience and political careers of new legislators are drastically different from those of *nomenklatura* elites. Before 1980, as many as 30 per cent of them were in various forms and to differing degrees involved in oppositional activity against the communist regime. In the years 1980–1 nearly 70 per cent of them were Solidarity activists and 50 per cent served at national and regional levels of the union. Moreover 15 per cent assisted Solidarity in various ways.

Nearly half of the legislators elected from the Solidarity list of nominees were interned or sentenced to prison after the imposition of marital law. Over a half (54 per cent) participated in the work of underground Solidarity in the years 1982–8 and another 4 per cent were associated with other organisations illegal at the time. Moreover a great portion (46 per cent) supported in various ways the fight of the democratic opposition through editorial and publishing work, charitable actions, participation in the committees for citizens' rights, ecological societies, Amnesty International and related organisations.

Throughout the period of their public activity a great number of MPs and senators elected from Solidarity lists of candidates (43 per cent) co-operated in various ways with the Catholic Church or organisations connected with it. This consisted of active participation in the Clubs of Catholic Intelligentsia, ministries for divergent *milieux* (for example, for college students), membership of various advisory bodies (such as Citizens' Primate Board) and commissions (for example, the Episcopate Commission for Legal Matters, the Polish Episcopate Commission for Charity), involvement in Church cultural and educational initiatives and so on. Some of the Solidarity MPs and senators (10 per cent) were also, during their pre-parliamentary time, associated with alternative political parties.

The biographies of Solidarity legislators show an entirely new picture of Polish society: they represent the large contingent which, at the time of communist dictatorship, had no chance of appearing on the public scene. At the same time they demonstrate a serious split within the Polish intelligentsia. Its two factions, one previously connected with the Party and entangled in various formal structures, and the other formerly driven to the margin of public life, coexist as if they belong to two different worlds which, it seems, cannot be reconciled by any means. This does not bode well for the future.

These CVs together show what a great departure has been made from the previous system of leadership recruitment. It is undoubtedly an important step towards the democratisation of social relations.

CONCLUSIONS: TOWARDS AN IDEAL MODEL OF ELITE RECRUITMENT

To return to the original subject of dilemmas and controversies associated with the patterns of leadership recruitment, it should be noted that the presented biographies provide evidence for a 'combatant' origin of the majority of MPs and senators. Is that to be an argument supporting the assumption of a *new nomenklatura*? One might well ask what different kinds of origin could these people possibly have had? Should Solidarity have promoted its opponents, or perhaps candidates of obscure political opinions? The salient feature of the new patterns of leadership recruitment should not be simply that the new elite includes representatives of new political groups. Rather the very process of recruitment should approach as closely as possible an *ideal model* of elite recruitment. Such an ideal model would be defined by postulating three requirements:

1. In the selection process the will of the majority should be observed: *the requirement of democracy.*
2. No collective body (professional, ethnic, religious, political or other) should be identified as ruling out access to the elite and one and all should have the same chances and observe the same rules: *the requirement of equality of social opportunities.*
3. Those people identified should be the best qualified to fulfil their roles, the most competent and those with as much experience as possible: *the requirement of meritocracy.*

    It is unnecessary to prove that the meeting of all three conditions can be extremely difficult and that no miraculous system exists which would automatically guarantee complete fulfilment of all of them. It seems equally unnecessary to remind anyone that in a communist regime none of these requirements was fulfilled: recruitment was not carried out in a democratic way and neither equality of social opportunity nor meritocractic conditions were observed.

It should be understood that in the Poland of today (as in Hungary and possibly other countries of Eastern Europe) the dilemmas connected with elite recruitment and, more generally, with overall personnel policy are quite different from those of a year ago. At that time the main goal was to establish the strongest possible and most consistent group (note, incidentally, called 'Wałęsa's *team*') able to challenge the experienced and strong *nomenklatura*. At that time nobody raised objections that it was not a group elected democratically and that it did not reflect fully the divergence of political opinions within society. Today, when the division between 'us' and 'them' is no longer applicable, the time has come for ever-present political differences to come out into the open. This is why today's controversies concerning leadership recruitment have emerged. The recommendation that he or she is one of 'ours' is not sufficient any more, because 'ours' now has not one, as was the case a year ago, but several meanings.

It should be realised that the process of leadership recruitment is a political one and it has to be conducted primarily through political structures. The basic element in those structures is formed by political parties and not by trade unions, or institutionalised social movements and citizens' initiatives, or other associations and religious groups. Obviously the latter categories do participate in politics and public life and nominate their representatives to various authorities and legislative bodies. But they cannot be substitutes for political parties. Therefore, as long as there exists no clear, fully-formed political structure in the post-communist countries, there will develop no stable or acceptably delineated model for elite recruitment.

Notes

1. In this study I make use of materials prepared in the course of research sponsored by the University of Warsaw Project, 'Political Culture of Polish Society'. The observations presented are not of a strictly academic nature but are rather the standpoint of an eyewitness who, being a sociologist, cannot avoid the expression of a scholarly outlook. Some of the themes presented have already been published: J. Wasilewski, *Społeczne procesy rekrutacji regionalnej elity władzy* (*Social Processes of Regional Power Elite Recruitment*) (Warszawa-Wrocław: Ossolineum, 1990); J. Wasilewski, 'The Patterns of Bureaucratic Elite Recruitment in Poland in the Seventies and Eighties', *Soviet Studies*, Vol. 42 (1990) pp. 743–57. In these studies one may find empirical arguments for many statements presented here as well as bibliographical references.

    In this chapter I refer to the phenomena occurring in Poland but it is my opinion that they apply to and are characteristic of other East European countries (hence the title). Generalisations on the leadership recruitment in Poland and other countries of the region (particularly Hungary and Czechoslovakia) were presented at international seminars in Dubrovnik

(April 1990), Budapest (May 1990) and Warsaw (Jabłonna, June 1990) at which scholars from East European countries noted the fundamental similarities of processes occurring in Poland to the ones happening in their countries.

2. In this chapter I use the term *'nomenklatura'* in its third sense. Whenever I am referring to the first sense, I speak of the 'system' or 'principle' of *nomenklatura*.

3. *Nasi w Sejmie i Senacie* (*Our People in the Diet and Senate*) (Warszawa: Oficyna Wydawnicza 'Volumen', 1990).

7 Between Hope and Helplessness: Women in the GDR after the 'Turning-point'

Irene Dölling

In October and November 1989, women in the GDR optimistically entered the public sphere with demands of their own. The active engagement of large numbers of women in grass-roots democratic initiatives, self-help, consciousness-raising and discussion groups was evident. At the beginning of December, the hope that women would henceforth become so vast a force that they could no longer be overlooked was strengthened when over a thousand women from throughout the GDR met in a large Berlin theatre and voted to found an Independent Women's Union. A few days later, representatives of the Independent Women's Union took their places as members of the Central Round Table. The Independent Women's Organisation participated in a joint election campaign with the Green Party and received 2.7 per cent of the vote. On the other hand, over 46 per cent of all registered women voters chose the 'Alliance for Germany'. These results were both disappointing and sobering. This voting behaviour, however, provides us with unexpectedly clear evidence for a number of conclusions regarding the situation of women in what is now the former GDR after the 'turning-point'.

First of all, it makes it distinctly clear that the vast majority of women in the GDR do not associate themselves with emancipatory or feminist ideas and practices and, in fact, reject them. The needs and behavioural structures of most women are obviously not what the Independent Women thought. The threat of unemployment, the unclear status of legal and property rights, vacillation on the question of a currency union and its already visible effects (high prices for food-stuffs, inflation) and so on have led to a deep insecurity on the part of almost all GDR citizens. Although women are affected specifically as women – for example, at this moment feminised job categories are especially threatened (women now make up more than 50 per cent of the unemployed and less than 25 per cent of those rehired) – they have offered hardly any resistance. Helpless outrage at what is happening to them and their families, or resigned acceptance of the brutal forms of discrimination and exclusion with which primarily men are now beginning to practice competition – these are 'normal' responses.

My thesis is as follows: under state socialism women developed subjective structures which provide fertile soil for 'conservative' solutions to the conflicts arising in the process of radical change on the path to a 'different modernism' (Ulrich Beck). The social 'achievements' of socialism must be examined critically from this perspective in order to understand the situation in which women of the GDR find themselves today.

Unfortunately there is no place in this chapter for discussing the question as to how really emancipatory or 'woman-friendly' were the conditions and social supports created for women under state socialism. Here can only be stated the following: formal legal equality, state measures and supports to allow women to combine career and motherhood, state programmes to raise women's level of education and qualifications to those of men, et cetera, were – until now – internationally recognised advantages and 'achievements' of socialism in the GDR. On the other hand we know very well that these conditions and social policy measures were not necessarily 'woman-friendly' or emancipatory, because women were regarded primarily functionally – as workers or as mothers – in these measures and not as subjects with a claim to self-determination and responsibility for their own lives. Nevertheless the mere statement of these facts and the contradictory effects of the social policy measures affecting working women with children is not sufficient to explain women's current wavering between hope and helplessness: their lack of power to resist the social cut-backs now beginning, on the one hand and the attractiveness of such traditional values as family, the roles of mother and housewife and so on to a not insignificant number of women, on the other.

To approach a clearer understanding of the underlying causes, it is in my opinion necessary to examine first, the general role of patriarchy in state socialism and its influence on women's behavioural structures. I propose to do this in a series of theses.

1. State socialism is a form of modern society characterised by the dominance of political policy over all other systemic structures. That is, the political system provides the representation of all other systems. Like the *pater familias* within the pre-bourgeois family-centred

production system, 'the Party', with its centralist–hierarchical structure led by its General Secretary as the 'Father of the Nation', takes over the function of speaking in the interest of the whole, of knowing what is good for everyone, as well as taking upon itself the responsibility for the welfare of all.

This patriarchal–paternalist principle merges with the political idea of a society of social equality and justice in the sense that the 'fatherly' Party, or State, assures justice and equality. This principle finds its expression, extension and stabilisation in the practical and symbolic gender order, which orders the daily life of the individual. This means that patriarchal structures can **never** become the object of critical reflection or practical change: under these conditions, criticism of patriarchal gender relations is direct criticism of the political system. Applied locally, individual efforts to depart from traditional gender roles and stereotypes becomes at best a 'purely personal', 'private' matter which cannot take on the quality of a public, institutionalised confrontation with patriarchal structures.

2.   Representation means the disqualification of those who are represented, and the repression of forms of a public political discourse and a 'civil society' in which independent, differentiated interests of those represented could be presented, articulated and developed. The lack of a women's movement in the GDR (and in all of the socialist countries) is thus in no way accidental. If women in the modern period have been at a general disadvantage because, since the nineteenth century, the constitution of a public political sphere has been a process primarily 'of a man's affair among men',[1] a reinforcement of this trend can be established within state socialism. This can be seen as a significant cause of the fact, that since October 1989, relatively few women have participated in the process of constructing a public political sphere in the GDR, and those few have been rapidly marginalised or have themselves withdrawn in resignation. Many of the women who became active in grass-roots organisations or in the old or new parties were forced to recognise that, after an 'open', 'euphoric' phase in the autumn of 1989, women's emancipatory claims did not carry very much weight in the developing struggle for the consolidation of political power. The distribution of positions is primarily a matter for men. The issue of gender quotas has not been mentioned in Parliament since the March 1990 election.

3.   Representation, however, also means relieving the individual of responsibility. The patriarchal–paternalistic principle generalises a cultural pattern taken from daily life: the father or man takes responsibility for the children or wife – which also gives him the right and

power to make decisions concerning them. Women in the GDR were until now integrated into full-time paid labour as well as having the responsibility for children and housework. This double and triple burden hardly left them room to escape the snares of a tutelary ideology, which was delivered to them free of charge – along with social welfare measures to increase the compatibility of work and motherhood. The grateful acceptance of dependency is 'inscribed into' this ideology. It may be that women in the GDR have, to a certain degree, overcome their dependence on their husbands through their paid labour, but they are caught at the same time in a dependency upon 'Father State', of which they are in most cases just as unaware as they are of their dependency on a husband – and to which they even consent.

I therefore suspect that behind the demands of many so-called 'normal', that is non-feminist women, for the guarantee of social policy 'achievements', there also lies a massive fear of the loss of a social welfare network which took care of them and their children or families, according to a traditional cultural pattern. This is also a massive emotional fear of a situation in which individual lack of responsibility will no longer be rewarded, but more responsibility for oneself will be demanded. In the current context of radical change, this behaviour pattern, created and spread by a patriarchal state socialism, makes women susceptible to parties which are ready to relieve them of their responsibility once again.

4. The lack of goods and services, as well as the previous absence of a competitive 'elbow society' led to the striking stability of traditional living groups under state socialism. The family (in the broadest sense), circles of friends and acquaintances, group solidarity and so on have acted in a form and with bonding power which, in West Germany for example, had begun to disappear in the 1950s.

One consequence of this is the conservation of traditional structures, especially gender roles and stereotypes. Despite their employment, most women have experienced their traditional role within the family as something they did not want to lose and have regarded it as their sphere of influence, not least because their paid work was frequently unskilled, monotonous, poorly paid and socially not as highly regarded as male work. This was also further reinforced by a 'Father State policy' which manifested itself in direct improvements in the quality of life as well as egalitarian social guarantees which an individual could definitely experience and evaluate positively.

All of this led to the fact that the majority of women in the GDR did not question their customary role in the family and regarded their employment primarily as a 'double burden' and not as a precondition for emancipation.

5. The subordination of the individual to a general concept has a further patriarchal dimension: certain aspects of common human interests are excluded *ex post facto*; 'human' interests, when looked at more closely, reveal themselves to be male. The 'builders of socialism' are of course male; women may take part in the process of socialist construction by 'working like a man'. Provided with an honorarium as a mother (preferably of three children), women play no role in public or publicised consciousness as the ones who perform by far the greatest part of unpaid household labour. As housewives they do not exist within the general concept of 'the socialist individual'.

Over several generations, women in the GDR have lived with and within a contradiction which demands of them all of the behaviours and qualities internal to the traditional women's role while at the same time either ignoring significant aspects of the skills and abilities which belong to this role or disqualifying them as socially unimportant. Women were supposed to behave in a traditionally 'female' manner while neither 'femininity' in the customary sense, nor the insistence on gender difference was recognised or honoured – women were supposed to work, think and develop their abilities 'like men'. This multiple devaluation may have nourished among many women the furtive wish to live out these discriminated dimensions of 'contextual female existence'. Now these longings can be openly articulated, and at the moment they conjoin with an emotional rejection of everything that was 'socialism'. The sudden attractiveness to many women of 'femininity' and 'motherliness' or even the vision of an existence without paid work, which has also manifested itself in women's acceptance of 'Miss' contests, sexist portrayals of women and so forth, must, in my opinion, be seen in relationship to the above-named symptomatic and affective methods of patriarchal state socialism.

Although I have been able to illustrate this problem only in a very shortened form, I hope that I have succeeded in establishing the beginnings of an explanation for the fact that the majority of women in the GDR, despite so many favourable conditions, have emancipatory demands – previously repressed – which can now burst forth.

The question of how the long-term effects of a 'heritage' of 40 years of state socialism and patriarchal–paternalistic policies will express themselves remains open. We will have to wait to see how former GDR citizens use their newly-gained freedoms within a bourgeois democracy, as well as what role their previous experience and former rights – for example, to economic security – will play. For now it is certainly realistic to assume that the specific manifestation of patriarchy within state socialism enouraged and stabilised, in the majority of individuals, behaviour and value structures which now provide a favourable basis for the transition to a modern society of the bourgeois–capitalist type. This transition is characterised by 'conservative' omens: for the above-named reasons, traditional projections of 'femininity' and the women's role exert an attraction for women; male dominance, never questioned within state socialism, provides men with a good launching-pad into the achievement-oriented 'elbow society' and for a first robust and unselfconscious application of their superior power to women. The majority of men and women want to achieve the West German standard of living as quickly as possible and are therefore deaf to references to limitations or delays along this path, required in the interests of equality of the sexes, a healthy environment or people in the 'third world'.

It is not at all out of the question that these 'conservative' preconditions may, in fact, be favourable to a rapid transition to a different modern society and to the mitigation of the social conflicts arising from it. The price, however, is high: much of what has been accomplished in the past decades in the interest of dismantling patriarchal gender relations and promoting the emancipation of women, laborious and inadequate as it has been, is now endangered *in the East and the West.* Achievements, already practically in hand, will probably be partially or totally lost; the Utopia of an equality within differences between the sexes will survive only in a small minority of cases; and it will be primarily women who pay the price. To be sure, improvements in the situation of women will in future be less a 'gift from above' than the result of women's own demands and struggles. Thus women will place a higher value on the fruits of their own efforts than on gifts, which generate dependency and for which gratitude is expected.

Note

1.   Karin Hausen, 'Thoughts on the gender-specific structural change of the public sphere', lecture at the congress 'Human rights have no/a gender', Frankfurt/Main 1989 (publication forthcoming).

8 Civil Society in Slovenia: From Opposition to Power
Tomaž Mastnak

'Civil society' is the concept that summarises the democratisation – or the transformation from totalitarianism to democracy – in Slovenia, as elsewhere in the socialist half of Europe.[1] As elsewhere, the concept implies a normative political philosophy, as well as describing and helping us to analyse and understand a wide range of empirical democratic struggles. The distinctive feature of the transformation to democracy in Slovenia, however, is that it was initiated by the new social movements (NSM) and that they – and not dissident intellectuals, or reform communists, or the aging New Left elite – played the crucial role in the formative period of civil society. The network they formed was called 'the alternative scene', or simply 'the alternative'.

Civil society was invented in 1983 in a seminar and happening, 'What is Alternative?', organised by the alternative scene in Ljubljana. By invention I mean the discovery of the term which intepretatively appropriated experiences of autonomous social activities from the second half of the 1970s on and designed a prospect of independent social action in the future.[2] To sum up, civil society was invented by the alternative, and the concept was first applied to its inventor – as an analytical model and as a political norm. The actors in the alternative scene – NSM in the first place – were understood as the main actors in the constitution of civil society, its institutions as the crucial institutions of the civil society in formation; and the alternative public sphere as the catalyst of the independent public.

It is important that civil society was initially conceived as alternative rather than opposition. As a sphere distinct from, independent of, and opposed to the sphere of state action, it was an alternative to socialism: to the existing socialist system as well as to the idea of socialism, including the idea of 'democratic socialism'.[3] It is true that it was first articulated as 'socialist civil society', but it was found very soon tht this term was a contradiction in terms. Socialism was understood as a project aiming to abolish the distinction between state and civil society in order to create an harmonious community. The state–civil society distinction, on the other hand, was postulated as a democratic norm and perceived as a necessary condition of democracy. In this sense, the reinvention of civil society was a rediscovery of democracy against the idea of socialism. In the given case, consequently, the distinction between state and civil society offered a starting-point from which to criticise and refute self-management as an anti-statist and anti-social project. By abolishing the difference between the state and civil society, it caused the state as well as civil society to wither away and created an amorphous system of domination and voluntary servitude. As such, self-management – as ideal and as reality – was a deformed creature, Leviathan and Behemoth at the same time.

The other consequence of conceiving civil society as alternative was understanding civil social action as positive activity: it preferred producing new, open, social spaces, creating alternative culture, independent public spheres and so on to confronting official structures or attempting to change them. To put it more precisely, it challenged the system symbolically and was, in this sense, in a system where politics was practised as repressive rather than symbolic – or communicative – action, 'anti-political'. With respect to Slovenia one could say that 'anti-politics' was the ethos of civil society in its formative period. As such, civil society might well have been called 'the other Slovenia' yet it has never been conceived as the would-be 'parallel *polis*' (alternative political system) of which Benda spoke in Czechoslovakia.

In this chapter I hope to describe (1) the formation of civil society in the late 1970s and early 1980s; (2) its politicisation, or the formation of political society in the second half of the 1980s; and (3) the first results of civil society in power in the 1990s.

STATE v. CIVIL SOCIETY

The first new social movement in Slovenia was punk. When it emerged in 1977, it was a youth subculture. Looking back we can understand it as the first attempt to build independent society. It was also the first major breach of the settlement established by the late president Tito and his 'soldiers of the revolution' (as the orthodox communists used to call themselves) who suppressed the liberalisation of the 1960s in Yugoslavia.

Protagonists of the movement, the first generation free from socialist ideology, renamed the world they lived in and created new cultural codes, '*altri codici*', to use Melucci's term. As ideology is the symbolic bond that holds society together, this first dissolution of socialist ideology somehow set society free. Punk in Slovenia not only proved that independent social life was possible, it invented the concept itself and created elements for the formation of a new social and political language. The response of authorities was police repression. It failed, and there are three main reasons for the failure. The first was the ability of the protagonists of the punk scene to enforce public discussion of the accusations invented by the police and disseminated by the mass media and thereby to displace the conflict from the repressive to the ideological level. The second resulted from the fact that, for the first time after a decade of intensified communist dictatorial rule, the ideological and political divisions carefully cultivated by the authorities to split the (critical) intelligentsia and fragment society were bridged over and a broader mobilisation of the independent public occurred – in a way, a 'democratic front' was formed – which condemned the 'anti-youth chauvinism' of the authorities in particular and the use of violence to solve social problems in general. The third reason was that the official youth organisation (ZSMS) gave in to pressure 'from below'; that is, it ventured to establish contacts with the critical and active segment of the young generation aggregated around the punk scene and listened to its arguments. It made possible a public discussion in which all concerned could take part.

As the police, especially the state security, were the stronghold of the old regime – in the most extreme case responsible to the highest party state leaders, the source of their knowledge and the executor of their will – the failure of the repression had far-reaching consequences. It opened up space for autonomous social activities. In the years that followed, 'proper' NSM emerged in the country: pacifist, environmentalist, feminist, gay, spiritual ('new age') ... By the mid-1980s NSM and youth subcultures formed an alternative network which remained for some time relatively submerged. The actors were mainly young people under eighteen, which points to the fact that the cultural revolution of the 1970s had successfully devastated the universities. Almost no students were involved, yet younger intellectuals who had already finished their studies played an important role. A number of the most able among them (some of whom could not get jobs at a university as they were declared 'morally–politically inappropriate'[4]) found their way to and their place in the alternative scene. Their great concern was to avoid the dangers of vanguardism. They became a group among other groups and produced the most dynamic political and social theory of the time as part of the alternative culture. This constellation contributed to a permanent self-reflection of the alternative and to its clear understanding of the social and political 'environment'; besides this, intellectuals had the skills to refute ideological and political attacks on the scene and to preserve an open space for its other protagonists in which they could articulate themselves.

A crucial role in the formation of the alternative scene was played by the local radio station, Ljubljana-based *Radio Študent* (Radio Student). Its programme linked broadcasting rock music with political analysis and theoretical discourse: out of this mixture of youth subcultures, criticism of totalitarian systems, 'post-marxism' and Lacanian psycho-analysis – to which very soon particular issues raised by pacifists and anti-militarists, gays, feminists and ecologists were added – sprang the new political culture. *Radio Študent* was important for creating a subtle sense of media. This led to the formation of alternative media: first independent publications (leaflets, fanzines, bulletins, records, tapes, books, videos) appeared in the alternative. Yet this was only a part of the story; not less decisive were the attempts to influence or take over official media. The greatest success in this respect was the trans-formation of the ZSMS' weekly *Mladina* (The Youth) which in the mid-1980s became the forum of the democratic civil society and soon after the most influential political magazine in the country. Some other – similarly marginal – media changed as well, but the central ones resisted new developments and remained closed to the new ideas. This meant that the editors-in-chief remained loyal servants to the power-holders who appointed them, which caused great discontent among journalists, a number of whom organised themselves and declared that they were responsible to professional ethics and not to the Party line.[5] In the mid-1980s, the official media monolith began to melt.

This was also the time when intellectuals of the middle generation began to become involved in the formation of civil society. A group of them, more of less established yet critical of the existing system and dissatisfied with their role in it, succeeded in founding an independent journal, *Nova revija* (The New Journal). This was perhaps the first major concession of the authorities, and the journal itself became one of the most influential oppositionalist publications. On the other hand, professional associations, like those of writers (close to *Nova revija*), sociologists and philsophers, reactivated themselves and contributed considerably to the 'rebirth of society'.

CIVIL SOCIETY v. CIVIL SOCIETY

The failure of police repression did not mean that the authorities had reconciled themselves to the emerging civil society. Its status remained insecure. NSM, the principal actors, had no possibility of being registered and legally recognised, which, so they hoped, could have protected them against arbitrary state repression. A solution was found in making a kind of contract with ZSMS. NSM formally became attached as collective members of ZSMS, without giving up their autonomy. Looking at this from the other side, ZSMS became the umbrella organisation for those movements, groups and initiatives. Both partners had their benefits: NSM gained legality and ZSMS created for itself a growing legitimacy. I would not interpret this symbiosis as an attempt to integrate NSM into the system, or as a form of surveillance over them, but rather as a decisive step towards transforming the system. With the giving-in of ZSMS, the political monolith began to fall apart. On the other hand, NSM, by their very existence, introduced pluralism: other subjects than the Party and its auxiliaries entered the scene and, besides this, a pluralism of forms of activity and forms of organisation emerged.

The new constellation, however, only caused a restructuring of repression aginst the key actors of independent society, and civil society proved to be an ambiguous phenomenon. If civil society is a *conditio sine qua non* of democracy it is not necessarily democratic itself. If there is no democracy without civil society it is still not impossible to imagine civil society without, or against, democracy. As the attempt to eliminate the first NSM by repressive state intervention failed (which could be seen as success for the emerging civil society) the state drew appropriate consequences. It gave up repression and handed it over to civil society.[6] The social violence concentrated in the state (to allude to a Marxian formula) was dispersed and given back to society; or the state transferred a part of its competence to civil society: violence was socialised and the state partially withered away.

Former state violence ceased to be political as soon as civil society internalised it. Previously directed against individual protagonists of the alternative scene, the violence now turned against the appearances of 'otherness' in public and aimed at the elimination of the social spaces of difference and otherness. Places specially designed for production and/or consumption of alternative culture were closed down one after another and it became increasingly difficult to rent places for performances; in this way the alternative population was fragmented and took refuge in bars, coffee-houses or restaurants, only to be driven away again (the places were closed down, reconstructed, imposed an entrance fee, their purpose was redefined, the personnel refused to serve punks and other unconventional clients, and so on). The alternative was forced constantly to migrate and after each migration it grew smaller, it became more fragmented and demoralised; the symbolic presence of the alternative in the city was systematically eradicated: grafitti writers were persecuted, graffiti erased, posters and notices torn down and so on. All these oppressive and repressive activities were clearly unpolitical, unplanned; nobody 'in the background' pulled the strings, it was all grass-roots. Reasons given for closing down the places were of a technical nature – urbanistic, traffic, hygienic, fire-preventive, earthquake-preventive, sound-proof isolation ... Everything was initiated, put into practice and executed by the people themselves, who hate those who look and behave differently, fearing AIDS, demanding quiet at night, complaining about urinating at street corners and so on. They acted in the name of the moral majority or as the *vox populi* instigating 'the responsible authority' to assume measures; they organised themselves as residents in neighbourhoods, as citizens in the local communities, as 'social owners' in public places or as workers in coffee-houses. They were the socialist consciousness and the nation's conscience synthesised. The attempted elimination of the social spaces of difference and otherness was an experience in 'direct democracy'. Civil society turned against its own democratic potentials. I call this phenomenon 'totalitarianism from below'.

Totalitarianism from below could not gain the upper hand, yet it has remained present as a feature of the rediscovered civil society which has to be taken into account. If it could not eliminate the alternative scene, that does not mean it has not had an impact on developments. In the mid-1980s the first major differentiation in civil society occurred. Elements of the independent social activities excluded themselves from the public, from the communicative exchange with 'society at large'. They gave up their striving to speak publicly and their expectations of being listened to, they ceased to refer to public discussions and common values, they chose speechlessness to be their language of communication with 'society'.[7] In this respect, they decided to be silent but refused to be silenced. They did not give up their activity, they just turned it inwards, dedicated it to themselves. Far from having to deal with a kind of quietism, we have to recognise a new logic of social activities. We have to deal with social activities which do not need an external adversary to constitute themselves and which, in their practice, therefore do not seek to negate the adversary's position but rather to grapple with their own internal deficiencies and insufficiencies. I have described this as 'the implosion of the social'.[8]

On the other hand, contrary to this silent and invisible, imploded civil society, totalitarianism from below, reactions to it and its only partial success led to an explosion of the social: civil society has definitively reappeared. Resistance to the attempt to eradicate the social spaces of difference and otherness, to eradicate differences and otherness from the social, initiated or intensified the struggle of major parts of the democratic civil society to establish their presence in public. They oriented their activities towards the public, presenting their programmes, ideas and concrete initiatives, reacting to the slander or accusations against them. In the mid-1980s, the first independent demonstrations were organised, numerous petitions, open letters and public statements written, a number of seminars held; feminists appeared in public, homosexuals organised the first week of gay culture in Ljubljana in 1984 and so on. The major success in popularising the alternative's ideas, however, was the peace movement's initiative for the recognition of conscientious objection and introduction of civilian service as an alternative to the military service.[9] It was furiously attacked by the army and (mainly federal or Serbian) political bodies yet it remained present in the media. The idea became known and along with it other ideas forming the social and political imagery of NSM. By 1986/7, the greater part of Slovene society had accepted them.[10]

What happened might be explained with the help of Kant's interpretation of the French Revolution. Kant, as is well know, saw the greatness of the revolution not in the event itself (in the revolutionary drama) but in the feelings of enthusiasm it aroused in those who were not directly involved, who were spectators of the historic spectacle:

> The revolution of the witty nation which has been taking place these days before our eyes might succeed or fail; it might be the cause of such misery and such atrocities that a well-intentioned man, were he in a position which would give hope to accomplish it successfully for a second time, would never take the decision to make the experiment at such a price – what I am saying is that this revolution invokes in the sentiments of all the spectators (who themselves are not involved in the play) the desire *to participate* which borders on enthusiasm and the expression of which means to take a risk, the cause of which could therefore be only a moral disposition in the human race.[11]

Kant recognised in this willingness, or desire, to participate the *signum rememorativum, demonstrativum, prognosticon*; that is the historical sign that testifies to the fact that humanity is progressing to the good. NSM under socialism or, more exactly, the enthusiasm they provoked in the people not directly involved, were such a *signum remorativum, demonstrativum, prognosticon.*

EMERGENCE OF POLITICAL SOCIETY

In 1985, the term 'civil society' first appeared in the discourse of the ruling party. This was a symptom of the Slovene League of Communists' (ZKS) changing attitude to the new reality. After the failure of repression, they had ignored NSM, hoping they were only a fashionable aping of Western counterparts which would soon pass. As they discovered this was a vain hope they began to look for ways to get hold of the new concepts and thereby to disarticulate the alternative. On the one hand, they tried to reintegrate civil society into Marxist political language, to interpret it with the help of Gramscian neomarxism, in order to prove that civil social issues were 'organically' or 'essentially' linked to the existing self-management project, that this model was in fact a genuine civil society coming true and that civil society in that sense was in fact the Party's programmatic aim. On the other hand, they proceeded with an ideological 'differentiation' of NSM, the core of the alternative, recognising them, in principle, as an understandable and positive phenomenon yet refuting as negative features all that was new about them, critical of the system or subversive of it; in short, all that would escape integration and pacification. It took some years of inner-party discussion for these ideas to take form, by which time the Party had realised that it was not competing for a concept but engaged in a 'struggle for the youth' (as the Party plenum in 1987 phrased it). And when it launched this struggle, the loss of the support of young people for its politics was already a *fait accompli.*

An event of decisive importance in this period was the ZSMS congress in 1986.[12] Quite unexpectedly, ZSMS departed radically and definitively from the role of a 'youth transmission party' designed for it by the party state. It declared itself an organisation in civil society based on the achieved level of social self-organisation understood as the only real basis of democratisation of the country. It ceased to be the umbrella organisation of NSM; rather it adopted the issues put on the agenda by NSM without destroying their autonomy. It tried to transform itself to facilitate closer collaboration with the movements and initiatives and more effective ways of dealing with their concrete problems. In this way the alternative scene obtained its counterpart in the political system.

The end of the political monolith, the loss of the support of youth for official politics and the development of a relatively strong and clearly articulated civil society compelled the Part and its allies to take steps towards reforms. On the one hand, the Party gradually got rid of the 'old guard' and cautiously started its process of transformation into a social democratic party. On the other hand, the Socialist Alliance of Working People (SZDL), a 'crypto-communist' popular front organisation, tried to integrate independent social groupings, offering them legitimacy if they agreed to work under its umbrella.

As a response to those developments a phalanx of the *ancien régime* was formed, with the Yugoslav People's Army (JNA) as its heart. There is evidence now that the military political police had started an operation against the process of democratisation (which was most articulated in) called *Mladost* ('youth' in Serbian) as early as 1985. This meant that the alternative scene was for years under the surveillance of the military police, who decided that NSM and other autonomous activities were 'anti-socialist'. The politicising generals induced the federal political authorities to make a statement that there was a 'counter-revolution' in Slovenia which then, in turn, empowered the army to act; early in 1988 a military intervention in Slovenia was planned.

In this context, a military trial was held in Ljubljana in summer 1988. Two editors of *Mladina*, a contributor, a figure of importance in the opposition, and a sergeant-major of JNA, Slovene by origin, were charged with betraying a secret military document. The military court found them guilty without ever having proved the case. It was a clearly political show-trial – blatantly violating a number of laws, procedures and the Slovene constitution – which aimed at the suppression of democratisation in Slovenia. This aim failed because of an unexpectedly strong and resolute social mobilisation and resistance. The reaction of the public to the arrests and the criminal prosecution was immediate, massive and energetic. A committee for the defence of the defendants, called the Committee for the Defence of Human Rights (CDHR), was founded in Ljubljana, to become the organisational centre of a nation-wide democratic movement. It had more than a thousand collective members, along with more than 100 000 individual members.[13]

THE ROAD TO POWER

CDHR was formed in a period in which a cycle of NSM, constituting the alternative scene, was coming to an end – they had been legalised, their ideas had become a common good and their issues a matter of public concern – and a debate started on their future. The first effect the repression and the organised resistance to it had on NSM was the suppression of this debate. The second major effect of the new constellation was that social resistance absorbed their remaining energies: all NSM joined CDHR and their most active protagonists began to play an important role in it. CDHR could never have had such success and would not have become the first really massive democratic organisation in the country after the war if NSM had not created the independent society. CDHR in fact successfully capitalised on the experience of the alternative, which, however, had – so to speak – to suspend its 'proper' activities when this happened.

CDHR also caused a complex shift in the structuring of independent activities. Contrary to the positive strategy of the civil society in formation, CDHR's activity was a negative one: a reaction to federal state repression. The major shift, however, was the shift from independent social to independent political activity. Formerly unpolitical or 'anti-political' autonomous activities were absorbed into politics. CDHR unified the field of action into a political field of action. The sphere of independent social activities somehow vanished: the emergence of the political opposition coincided with the disappearance of the opposition to politics. On the other hand, CDHR's existence and activity decisively pluralised the political space. This was, however, a frustrated pluralism: the political space was only bipolarised, with CDHR on the one side and the weakening official politics on the other. The effect of this differentiation of political space – or the price for it – was the homogenisation of the independent sphere. This happened more easily because the threat to democratisation in Slovenia came from outside, from Belgrade. The defence of democracy, the nation-wide democratic movement, assumed nationalist form. The cause of democracy was linked to the question of national sovereignty.

There is yet another feature of these developments. CDHR was founded to help the *Mladina* defendants: the goal of its activity was purely legalistic, unpolitical. It was the unpolitical platform which attracted and unified numerous individual and collective members. So it happened that people of the most diverse political orientations joined forces and worked together. However the logic of the space in which CDHR was formed and had to conduct its activities compelled it to act politically. CDHR became a political organisation without ever having had a political platform. So it became a political organisation in which the members had to suppress their political identity. With regard to NSM this meant that they ceased to be social movements and had to give up dealing with their own particular issues. They had lost their identity twice without being in a position to develop a political identity.

Owing to the mass mobilisation structured around CDHR, the democratisation process in Slovenia was saved. As this became clear, the structural tensions created inside CDHR were set free: political identities were gradually articulated. In the autumn of 1988, the process of forming political parties started. Its background was the growing autonomy and strength of civil society as well as its inner differentiation and pluralisation which created the need for political representation. The forces of socialist self-management resisted this process yet, step by step, they had to make concessions. As it became clear that political pluralism was inevitable – unless a total blockade of social dynamics was risked, which was not a viable option at a point when the development of socialism had exhausted all its resources – they argued for a 'non-party political pluralism'. In the end even the SZDL, the most ardent advocate of this idea, transformed itself into a party and stood for elections, in spring 1990. The same happened to ZKS: the Party transformed itself into a party and made a considerable contribution to the peaceful transition from totalitarianism to parliamentary democracy.

I would like to point to three moments which, more than others, constituted this political transition, which could be conceived as demonopolisation of power. Firstly, ZSMS declared a 'struggle for power' in 1988. In the eyes of the communist rulers (who claimed that they had the historical mandate to govern) the 'struggle for power' was a deadly sin – this used to be the final accusation against their opponents. When ZSMS declared that it was struggling for power this not only meant that it refused to obey 'Big Brother'; it was already a redefinition of the nature of power. Secondly, ZKS, on the other hand, began to talk about its 'descent from power' more or less during the same period. It recognised that its monopoly of power was generating the crisis and at the same time blocking any attempt to solve it and was, consequently, a dead end; it also realised that it had to share power in order not to lose it altogether. What both processes, or declarations, have in common is the modern–democratic concept of power as an 'empty space'.[14] Both strategies have contributed to the constitution of democratic political space.

The third moment hinged on a kind of round-table talk in spring 1989. These talks have their own history. The CDHR had already established regular contact with the authorities who, for the first time, recognised a declared oppositional organisation as a dialogue partner.

Although the results of these contacts were relatively unsatisfactory for both sides, the ice was broken. The next event of major importance was a meeting held in Ljubljana early in 1989. In Stari trg in Kosovo, 1300 Albanian miners went on hunger strike, deep in the pits, to protest against the plan of the Serbian leadership to suspent the autonomy of the province.[15] As the local, Serbian and federal authorities refused to talk to the miners, even after the strike had been going on for a week and the lives of the strikers were seriously endangered, a group of people from the Slovene alternative scene decided to organise a meeting in solidarity with the miners and in protest against the irresponsible behaviour of the political authorities. The motive was to do something to save the miners' lives. All the opposition groups and the official political organisations in Slovenia joined the initiative and their highest representatives made speeches at the meeting. This was the first joint political action by the oppositionists and the officials. The Serbian leadership was infuriated, calling people onto the streets and threatening that this 'State and Party mob' would come to Ljubljana in order to prevent such an 'occupation'; the protagonists of the solidarity and protest meeting, nonetheless, decided to keep on meeting and to co-ordinate their activities. As the danger of the 'Serbian occupation' passed, meetings of this co-ordinating body focused on the political future of Slovenia. This was the beginning of the end of the meetings, mainly as a result of the SZDL's ambition to keep everything in its own hands.

The opposition was *de facto* legalised in this way; *de jure* legalisation was soon to follow: the law on political organisation was passed later that year. In spring 1990, free elections were organised in Slovenia. Five opposition parties – later joined by two further minor parties – formed a coalition called Demos (the Democratic Opposition of Slovenia). ZKS (who had by that time split from the Yugoslav League of Communists, dominated by anti-reformist forces, and changed its name to the Party of Democratic Renewal) and SZDL (who split into a faction of former officials and a faction of younger politicians and intellectuals who wished to form a modern socialist party on the ruins of the old communist transmission-belt organisation) formed the socialist bloc. ZSMS, which had transformed itself into the Liberal Party, decided to stand for election alone.

The elections, of course, have decisively shaped recent social and political developments.[16] First of all, intellectuals of the middle generation entered political life en masse. only a small number of them were the regime critics who at the beginning of the 1980s had founded *Nova revija*; others were people who had been sympathetic to their ideas yet held back from any public activity in the years of communist rule and in the critical period of the transition, and now felt the time had finally arrived for them to speak their minds and become involved in something which transcended the private sphere. In addition there appeared on the scene men (and maybe a woman or two) who, realising that a new power elite was in formation, calculated that it was the right time to take a share in power without risking anything; some of them were deserters from the old power elite, others became 'political men' for the first time. The ideologists of this new political formation first appropriated the term 'alternative' (at the time they had not yet found it convenient to describe themselves as 'opposition') and ultimately presented themselves as *the* democratic opposition. The former move rendered the 'historical' alternative nameless and, consequently, squeezed it out of political existence (which cannot be but symbolic), while the latter made it impossible for all the democratic oppositional groupings who had not joined Demos to call themselves 'democratic opposition'.

Secondly, NSM – the principal actors in the democratic civil society – remained suspended. On the one hand, they were unable to recuperate after the military trial episode and, on the other, their modes of action did not fit the model of competitive party democracy; that is, they were non-competitive. Moreover their protagonists realised that no political party could deal with their issues satisfactorily and, under the influence of the more fundamentalist views, having failed to form an electoral alliance with ZSMS, decided to stand for elections as the Independent List of NSM – which was badly defeated. The gradual demobilisation of the democratic civil society was, however, complemented by mobilisation of those parts of civil society which could be described as politically and democratically underdeveloped. This further meant that the new ideologist played a much greater role than they would have done in a politically more articulated *milieu*.

Thirdly, the success of Demos, by claiming it was more than a coalition of parties and that it represented nothing less than the general interest of the nation, was that it bipolarised the political space. ZSMS was played out, its fault being that it used to be an 'official' organisation under the old regime and was suspected of remaining a communist succursal. Its still more fatal sin was that it had not joined Demos, who reimposed the standard 'Who is not with us, is against us' (and 'Who is against us, is against the Nation'). In this way, by suppressing the past and present role of ZSMS (and, still more radically, that of NSM), Demos hoped to appropriate and monopolise the history of the opposition to the old regime. Once this was done, it could build its political strategy on anti-communism. On the other hand, the only positive programme it was able to offer was nationalism. The reduction of the struggle for democracy to the primitivism of anti-communism and the appealing simplicity of nationalism was the basis of Demos's electoral success.

CIVIL SOCIETY IN POWER

In the elections Demos got about 55 per cent of votes. The two strongest single parties in the Parliament, however, are the reform communists and the ZSMS–Liberal Party. The third-strongest party turned out to be the Christian Democrats, which was an unpleasant surprise for the ideological core grouping of Demos, the Slovene Democratic Alliance, which had assumed that they would win the election. The results, nevertheless, seemed to offer a good starting-point to found a democratic political system. Even if one assumed Demos won on an anti-communist vote, the communists – the Party of Democratic Renewal – were not eliminated from political life, although they had lost power. This was, in my view, advantageous for future democratic development because the communists are part of the political reality and their elimination would give a distorted picture of it, and because their participation in the new political order would guarantee (given their role in the transition process) a gradual development of a democratic parliamentary system. The fact that Demos won with a minimal majority seemed to lessen the dangers – and temptations – of the formation of a new monopolistic power, while its victory made possible the deconstruction of the old one. Finally the relative electoral success of the ZSMS–Liberal Party meant the presence of a third political bloc (still sensitive to NSM and their issues) and, consequently, the representation of an element of a pluralist, not just dualist, political space. On the basis of the electoral results one would have expected that power would be divided and shared by all the relevant political forces in the country. These expectations, however, proved vain.

Demos has so far worked at uncompromisingly creating a new monopolistic and monistic power structure. The negotiations between Demos's representatives and other political parties failed because Demos refused to make any concessions and insisted on having all the leading and decisive posts in its hands. The result is that the three branches of power are, once again, in the hands of one political formation. Most interesting is its behaviour in the Parliament. First it curbed the independent political functioning of its constitutive parties, somehow suspending their independent particular political identities and claiming that it was the unmediated embodiment of the general, that is, national interest. Its first act in the Parliament was to discipline its own MPs. Although its leaders advocated secret ballots as long as they were in opposition, they suspended them when they gained power so that they could have 'their' MPs under control. They transformed them into a voting machine which could, by their numerical strength, outvote any proposal of the opposition without having to argue against it. This kind of party discipline of a supra-party political corporation, of course, rules out politics founded on public discussion. It also tends to transform the Parliament into an executive body of the Demos leaders.

The second act of Demos's leadership in the Parliament was to turn down the Liberals' proposal that MPs should be paid for their work by the state. The demagogic explanation of the new rulers was that they wanted to reduce the costs of the state apparatus. In fact they sapped the material basis of the opposition parties, whose electoral success should have enabled them to work normally.[17] (The old sources of financing were abolished, and living on membership fees is almost impossible when parties are only taking shape after half a century of suppression of political pluralism). On the other hand, Demos themsleves decided to employ their own MPs within the state apparatus, which they now regarded as their property. In this way they have turned the elected 'representatives of the people' into their state employees, mainly of the executive power. What has been founded after the free elections is a new structure of political patronage and a new clientele. If one takes into account the fact that the new power is also trying to control the media, that it is – so far mainly by cutting state subsidies – remodelling culture and planning a purge of managerial structures, one could hardly escape the impression that we have got a revolution instead of democratic changes.[18]

These developments are, in my opinion, a general feature of post-communist Eastern Europe. I would not argue that the democratic project initially based on the notion of civil society, and practically rooted in self-reconstituted civil society, was betrayed. On the contrary, the present outcome is intimately connected to the original project. What we have now is civil society in power. Logically, civil society itself is without any limits. Its limits could be defined only in relation to the state. Civil society, in drawing limits to the sphere of state action, is defining its own limits as well. The state–civil society distinction implies limits both to the state and to civil social power. Civil society in power represents unlimited power. What was new about the democratic opposition to the old regimes was that it defined its own limits, it was the idea of self-limitation. What has been lost now is not the purity of civil society but the limits of political action and power of the victorious civil society. The state–civil society distinction, the great achievement of the oppositionist democratic politics of the late 1970s and 1980s, is disappearing again. It is disappearing with the victorious success of this politics. At this point the triumph of democratic political strategy turns into an installation of undemocratic power. If the destruction of civil society by the party state was the origin of the totalitarianism of the old regimes, in the new regimes, civil society in power might breed new totalitarianism.[19]

Notes

1. For the reinvention of civil society in Eastern Europe, see Andrew Arato, 'Civil Society against the State: Poland 1980–81' *Telos*, No. 47 (Spring 1981) and 'Empire vs. Civil Society: Poland 1981–82', *Telos*, No. 50 (Winter 1981–2); John Keane, 'Introduction', in Keane (ed.), *Civil Society and the State. New European Perspectives* (London/New York: Verso, 1988).

2. I would also like to point to 'external' influences: our discussions were inspired, on the one hand, by East European experiences (the Solidarity movement in Poland, especially, enjoyed great sympathy, and support as well; progammatic discussions of the Czech and Hungarian democratic opposition were also held and, on the other, mainly by the 'post-Marxist' debates and NSM in the West.

3. A Hungarian oppositionist compared democratic socialism to the wolf in 'Little Red Riding Hood'. See György Dalos, *Archipel Gulasch, Die Entstehung der demokratischen Opposition in Ungarn* (Bremen: Donat & Temmen Verlag, 1986) p. 131.

4. 'Moral-political appropriateness' was a clause imposed in the 1970s to purge public offices of the people who were not on the 'Party line'; it is the Yugoslav counterpart of the *Berufsverbot* and was widely practised until recently, despite the fact that it blatantly violated the rights guaranteed by the Constitution. It is still practised in the Kosovo province to eliminate all those who are not willing to submit unreservedly to the Serbian dictatorship.

5. The so-called Belgrade trial could be considered an important turning-

point. A group of Slovene journalists brought the authors whose reports from the trial prejudged the guilt of the defendants to the Court of Honour where they were found to have violated the professional code. The verdicts of the Court of Honour were published and from that point on the coverage of the trial in the Slovene press improved. This was a great moral victory and of importance for proving that limits could be set to the political diktat in the media as well as to political arbitrariness in the legal sphere.

6. I discuss this in detail in Mastnak, 'Modernization of Repression', in Vera Gáthy, (ed.), *State and Civil Society: Relationships in Flux* (Budapest: Hungarian Academy of Sciences).

7. The term 'speechlessness' is used by the German journal *Alternative*; see 'Indiz "Sprachlozigheit", *Alternative* 25 (1982) No. 142.

8. See my 'The Implosion of the Social Beyond Radical Democracy', in Tomasž Mastnak and Rado Riha (eds), *The Subject in Democracy* Ljubljana: MŠ ZRO SAZU.

9. The case is discussed in Gregor Tomo, 'Alternative Politics. Example of the Initiative for Civil Service', in Gáthy, *State and Civil Society.*

10. In 1986/7, opinion polls already reported that about 45 per cent of the Slovene population would participate in NSM, while about 75 per cent were sympathetic to their ideas and actions.

11. Immanuel Kant, *Der Streit der Fakultäten* (1794), Part II, 6 (see Kant, *Werkausgabe*, Vol X (Frankfurt/M: Suhrkamp, 1968) p. 358.

12. I report on the congress in '"Even the future is not what it used to be"', *Across Frontiers*, Vol. 3 (1988) No. 3.

13. I discuss the trial and the social resistance in 'The Night of the Long Knives', *Across Frontiers*, Vol. 4 (1989) No. 4 – Vol. 5 (1990) No. 1; see also Sonia Licht and Milan Nikolić, 'Endless Crisis', *Across Frontiers*, ibid.

14. See on this Claude Lefort, *L'invention démocratique* (Paris: Fayard, 1981) and *Essais sur la politique, XIXe–XXe siècles* (Paris: Seuil, 1986).

15. Now, a year later, it is clear that Serbia has in fact not only abolished the autonomy of the Kosovo province but established an apartheid-like regime. The Albanians who form nearly 90 per cent of the local population have been downgraded to second-class citizens, deprived of political representation, removed from leading posts in industry and cultural institutions; their rights and liberties have been suspended; segregation on an ethnic basis has been imposed in schools and the workplace and even in public transport. State terrorism, executed by the Serbian police, and (as it is reported) assisted by the army, with dozens of people killed, huge numbers of arrests, political justice, poisoning of schoolchildren and so on is what a great number of Belgrade politicians and media call the rule of law in Kosova.

16. For general observations on this question, see Andrew Arato, 'Revolution, Civil Society and Democracy', paper presented at the seminar, *The Present and Future Role of Party/State Apparatus in Peaceful Transition from Dictatorship to Democracy*, Budapest, 9–11 May 1990.

17. *Demokracija*, the pro-government paper which calls itself independent, has recently named the opposition 'the illegal power'.

18. On the reappearance of 'revolution' in Eastern Europe, see Arato, 'Civil Society vs. the State'.

19. An earlier version of this appeared in *Studies in Comparative Communism*, vol. 23, Nos. 3–4 (autumn–winter 1990).

9 Civil Society at the Grass-roots: A Reactionary View
Chris Hann

The perspective of a social anthropologist on the large issues addressed in this volume is very different from that of the other contributors. In this chapter I am concerned with the adequacy of concepts such as democratisation and civil society for an understanding of contemporary social transformations in Eastern Europe. Focusing upon a Hungarian community which I have known over the last 15 years, I shall argue that more attention should be paid to the needs and anxieties of citizens as they themselves express them in the context of their experiences under socialism. It seems to me that the discourse of civil society, particularly when linked to an extreme model of market economy, is an ideological product alien to most citizens. Many villagers regret the passing of an age when dogma and ideology were less obtrusive in their community and posed less of a threat to their welfare.

The rhetoric of civil society was widely used by Eastern European intellectuals in the 1980s, aided and abetted by influential commentators in Western countries.[1] One of the few authors to offer useful guidance in making the concept operational in social research is the Hungarian Elemér Hankiss, who points to the decline in the number of voluntary associations, particularly interest group associations, as evidence of the 'demobilisation' and 'atomisation' which occurred in the socialist period. Hankiss also tends to interpret the ebullient 'second economy' of Kádár's Hungary as contributing to exaggerated individualism, the alienation of citizens and their withdrawal from public life (though he also thought this sector might contain seeds of more humane and sociable resolutions to the most basic problems of social values and cohesion). The main implication is that a healthy society is spun upon the multiple webs of spontaneous formal associations, whereas the imposition of a single monolithic web under socialism made a decent society impossible.

Like Hankiss I am concerned in this chapter primarily with Hungary. Some of the arguments have a degree of validity elsewhere in Eastern Europe – mainly in parts of Poland and Yugoslavia – but conditions in, for example, Ceauşescu's Romania were of course entirely different. During most of the Kádár period Hungarian socialism was not based upon ideological dogma, but rather upon pragmatic policies which gave citizens considerable scope to pursue their ambitions as consumers. Hungarian society was transformed by these policies, for which it is difficult to find a simple label. The term *polgárosodás* is one which many Hungarians themselves might accept. It is usually translated as embourgeoisement, *polgár* corresponding both to 'bourgeois' and 'citizen'. But clearly the transformation which has taken place has not followed the bourgeois course on which Hungary had barely embarked in the pre-socialist period. Perhaps a better English equivalent would be 'modernisation'. Thus millions of rural citizens have become more dynamic producers of agricultural commodities, acquired new homes with electricity and bathrooms, and gained access to state-provided education and health care. This sort of material progress may constitute the essence of *polgárosodás* for many people, even when it is accompanied by a severe diminution of the free, autonomous associations found in abundance before 1948.

It is now conventionally assumed that the succession of partial reforms which began in the mid-1960s and continued, with occasional interruptions, until the socialists gave up power in 1990, was fundamentally flawed. So far as the economic arguments are concerned I am unconvinced. It seems to me that the main cause of later difficulties was a period of excessive borrowing in the 1970s, but this was an unnecessary extravagance rather than an integral part of the reforms. Meanwhile the real benefits of socialist modernisation were experienced by millions. Kádárist pragmatism was never especially attractive in political terms, nor should we overlook the periodic resurfacing of socialist dogmatism. But for the most part the pragmatists prevailed, enabling the majority of citizens to improve their living standards dramatically, among them many of the poorest and least integrated sections of the rural population. It is to such a rural community that I now turn.

Few inhabitants of Budapest (population around two million) have even heard of Tázlár (population around two thousand), a settlement on the flat sandy soils between the rivers Danube and Tisza, only a short drive from the Yugoslav border. Better known nationally is the larger neighbouring village of Soltvadkert, whose prominence in the wine trade is widely associated with the diligence and ingenuity of the Swabian Germans who have for centuries formed the community's most salient ethnic group. Tázlár itself was not settled intensively until late in the nineteenth century and its population was extremely diverse in ethnic and religious terms as well as economically.[2] In the socialist period pressure was applied to abandon the scattered farms on which most of these immigrants lived in favour of new residences in the nuclear centre. There has also been significant expansion of infrastructure and public building, including new churches, council offices and collective farming buildings.

To understand why I claim that this village epitomises the general thrust of pragmatist policies in Kádár's Hungary it is important to understand local farming practices. Tázlár, Soltvadkert and numerous other villages of the county were not obliged to form Soviet-style (*kolkhoz*) collective farms. Aware of the very negative reaction displayed by peasants towards such farms in the 1950s and afraid of very large economic losses, the authorities allowed many wine-producing communities instead to form associations known as 'specialist co-operatives'.[3] The essence of these co-operatives was a fudge. Theoretically when one joined (and joining was compulsory for most villagers, here as elsewhere) one signed over one's land to the co-operative and joined a collective organisation. In practice most farmers carried on as before, working their 'own lands' and retaining full ownership rights over their orchards and vineyards. It was underlined from time to time, right up to the 1980s, that the specialist co-operative was a transitional form of collective, which would in time move towards the model represented by state farms and *kolkhoz*-style collective farms. A certain amount of land was brought under collective cultivation at the outset and the specialist co-operatives were supposed to increase the proportion of such lands in the longer term. However most of their efforts were related to the stimulation of productions in the small farms of their members, who in the Tázlár region engaged in significant dairy production and pig raising as well as viticulture. This stimulation included help with inputs and machine services, as well as assistance in the marketing of produce. Behind this 'symbiosis' of small- and large-scale operations in agriculture lay the power of the socialist state.[4] Not only was this 'deviant' form of co-operative tolerated over the years (against ideologues suspicious in principle of the survival of family farming) but in the Tázlár case significant subsidies were enjoyed as a result of the relatively poor agricultural endowment of the village.

When my fieldwork began in the mid-1970s, the Tázlár co-operative was experiencing many economic difficulties, its leadership was highly unstable, and it was very far from popular with most of the membership. Yet in spite of these problems many farmers were becoming very prosperous, the village was experiencing a building boom, rates of car ownership were already higher than in urban Hungary, and all this in an area which had been one of the poorest before the socialist period. Farmers complained about their co-operative, particularly if it threatened to acquire their own land for socialist sector development schemes (whenever this happened compensation was offered; that is, alternative holdings elsewhere) but, unlike farms in, say, the Soviet Union, most of them were not subject to its hierarchical relations. Rather they exercised control themselves over what products they produced and in what quantities. For example, when the price of pork was not raised in line with expectations in the mid-1970s, small farmers nationally began to withdraw from this branch of production. Alarmed at the consequences of a shortage of meat the government soon raised prices and production resumed. This episode suggested to me that one could speak of a kind of 'market socialism' operating here, in the sense that the authorities did not attempt to dictate to small farmers what they should produce, but dealt with them indirectly through price signals. It should perhaps be emphasised that this was in no sense a 'free market' and the state always played a decisive role in the determination of these prices.[5]

The specialist co-operatives varied greatly in their achievements. In Soltvadkert they were very popular with members from the outset and were soon able to finance more ambitious collective investments, which in turn created more profitable opportunities for small farmers. But even in Soltvadkert they could not be expected to usher in a Western-style pluralist democratic society. In Tázlár, historically a less integrated community, alongside the increased evidence of private prosperity there were bitter divisions within the co-operative membership and in every sphere of public life. The political institutions were held in particularly low esteem. The council chairman in the 1970s was of poor peasant origin and widely reputed to be corrupt, only giving the go-ahead for rural electrification schemes after the appropriate bribe had been paid. He was also thought to be ineffectual in securing public funds for local development. In spite of the building of a large Culture House in the 1960s I also found that cultural life in the village had become stultified if not entirely stagnant by the 1970s. With religious denominations strictly excluded from any secular role and no other autonomous organisations of significance active in the public space, one might suggest that the dynamic energies of the community in this period were overwhelmingly channelled towards private accumulation. Such a hypothesis appears fully consistent with the arguments of

Hankiss. It can be assessed more fully if we move now to consider the developments of recent years.[6]

In all the instant mythologising which followed the revolutionary upheavals of 1989 in Eastern Europe it is often forgotten just how far Hungary had already travelled down the road of reform before this date. In Tázlár the appointment of a non-communist chairman of the specialist co-operative in 1982 was a landmark, bringing to an end an era of leadership instability characterised by repeated interventions by the external authorities. The new chairman was a qualified agronomist of Soltvadkert origin and the rest of the decade witnessed significant economic consolidation in the co-operative. Farming operations were streamlined and initiatives taken to create new jobs in non-agricultural activities (small factories employing mainly female labour in manufacturing shoes and plastic bags). Most of the co-operative's machine park was privatised through sale to employees, who then entered into contractual agreements with the co-operative and competed for business with other private tractor owners. The outstanding new investment was one which replicated a pattern pioneered previously in many other specialist co-operatives for new vineyards. Modern methods were used, thus permitting certain operations to be performed by machine, but in order to realise the benefits of family labour ownership rights were allocated to individuals. Both the costs and the eventual proceeds were shared between the co-operative and the individuals concerned, and significant state aid was also available to facilitate these investments. Studies have shown that the yield in such 'private members' joint farms' (*tagi közös*) can easily reach double that of an equivalent area of collective vineyard without such devolution of ownership and cultivation rights.[7] All these moves were examples of Kádárist pragmatism towards the rural population and they helped to win the specialist co-operative wider respect in the community.

Outside the co-operative there was little to match this dynamism. On the political front the former council chairman was by the mid-1980s a broken man, having received a suspended gaol sentence for corruption. He was replaced by the headmaster of the village primary school, who resigned from the (always minuscule) local cell of the communist party shortly afterwards. By 1990, this man was letting it be known that he favoured the restoration of religious instruction in state schools, as the only way to ensure adequate moral training for youth. However the churches were by no means well supported in Tázlár in the 1980s. The Roman Catholics who comprised the largest congregation were bitterly divided following a personal rift between the parish priest and the community's long-serving female cantor. After an unsuccessful appeal to the Bishop for a new priest the absence of the apathetic majority was augmented by a boycott on the part of the devout minority.

The new council chairman was widely respected for his work as director of the village Culture House, though he was the first to admit that this was a fairly thankless task.[8] Officially sponsored organisations such as the Women's Club attracted only small numbers to their perfunctory meetings. Perhaps the most active formal association in Tázlár in the 1980s was the Hunting Association. As elsewhere in Hungary, this had tended to attract some co-operative officials and included a significant number of communist party members.[9] But, by 1990, this too had disintegrated owing to a failure to agree on new officers and the Tázlár association was swallowed up by the larger association in Soltvadkert.

There was thus a continuing dearth of local associations or corporations when Tázlár residents went to the polls in 1990, first in the spring to elect a new parliament, and second in the autumn to elect a new mayor and local council. The revived Smallholders' Party had a strong base in this region and one of the leading activists was a Tázlár resident who looked set at one stage to become the party's parliamentary candidate. In the end he stepped down in favour of a better-known and respected vet, who was comfortably elected. During the summer of 1990, when I was back in the village, the Smallholders' Party was maintaining its high profile. Certainly no other party seemed well established, although several had a small core of activists (these were the Socialist (ex-communist) Party, the Christian Democratic People's Party, and the Agrarian Alliance; neither the Hungarian Democratic Forum nor the Free Democrats, the largest political forces in the country, were able to organise in Tázlár). The Smallholders' major symbolic victory came when they took over the space in the village council offices previously reserved for the communist party and had their emblem displayed in the window.

It is perhaps not surprising that there was strong support for the Smallholders' Party in a region in which family farming had retained its vitality thanks to the specialist co-operatives. But there were also deep paradoxes here, which came more into the open by the time of the local elections in September 1990. At one level there were plenty of voters ready to respond to certain elements of the Smallholders' message, and in particular the promise to create fully independent family farmers on the basis of the land owned by the family in 1947. To implement this principle literally implied the dismemberment of the specialist co-operative. The activists certainly saw matters in these terms, and it is no accident that some of them belonged to the families which stood to gain most from the policies of '1947 restoration'.

However it seems likely that many of those who voted a Smallholder into parliament in May 1990 were reluctant to elect a Smallholder as village mayor five months later. The local campaign was obviously exciting, though the account which follows is, regrettably, based largely on correspondence. In conversation in August 1990 the founder of the Smallholders' local organisation in the village was very honest about personal rivalries among the activists, and also about deep-seated reservations concerning the Smallholders' programme throughout the community. He complained that, although he always found massive support for his radical programme when he canvassed farmers individually, when he spoke out agains the co-operative leadership at a public meeting his support had melted away. He attributed this to a 'duality' (*kettősség*) in the nature of his fellow-villagers, rooted in the diverse traditions of their community, which made it very hard for them to accept a leader from within, from among themselves.[10] Indeed there was a fair amount of unpleasant gossip and slander about this would-be leader. His descent from a family which had been active in local administration before the socialist period carried no particular weight. Criticism focused on his lack of education, and on the fact that he did not even farm seriously himself and had virtually given up his occupation as a private motor mechanic in order to devote himself to researching the early history of the community. His family life (his wife, a former accountant at the co-operative, had died of cancer only a year earlier) was also placed under the microscope and found wanting by local opinion.

Other contenders for the new post of mayor experienced similar treatment: if X had the right educational background he could not understand the needs of ordinary farmer, or if Y could, then he had a worrying drink problem, and so on. There was general surprise that the out-going council chairman did not stand for mayor (he was easily elected as an ordinary councillor) and in the end six candidates had their names put forward. The most extraordinary campaign was run by a local entrepreneur, standing as an Independent. Possessing neither inherited wealth nor a prestigious name nor any impressive paper qualifications, this man had managed to build up a dynamic restaurant business in the 1980s, with interests which spread into neighbouring communities. However there were many adverse comments about some aspects of this 'success story'. For example, various rumours circulated following a fatal drugs incident at one of his restaurants. This candidate's manifesto emphasised his local origins and his intention to use the office of mayor to promote community development in vigorous and radical new ways. He would commission a new village emblem and publish a local history monograph. He would build new roads and negotiate with foreign capital to open a petrol station in the village. He promised to open up new marketing avenues for local farmers in Budapest and even in Austria. He would organise 'market research' to determine the priorities for commercial development within the community, and he even floated a scheme for an independent local bank. There was no mention whatsoever in this manifesto of the future of the specialist co-operative. This entrepreneur also summed up the message of numerous sociological studies of contemporary Hungary when he stated proudly in his manifesto that hitherto he had preferred not to get involved in local politics because 'I know just two important things, family and business, and I've devoted all my time to these two areas.'

Victory went by a large margin to another Independent, the socialist council's retiring executive secretary, a woman who had married into the community, had worked in socialist local administration since the 1950s, and was thought to favour strengthening the specialist co-operative rather than dissolving it. The entrepreneur would not accept the result. He took his objections through several stages of increasingly acrimonious appeal and gained national publicity, but all to no avail. (According to my informants, if anyone was guilty of electoral malpractice it was he, for his services to voters were by no means confined to offers of transport to the polling booths.) It is obvious that much bitterness was generated (according to one letter the village was 'like a wasp's nest' for months afterwards) and I tell the story of these elections in detail so that the reader may understand how difficult it is in a place like Tázlár to establish the basis of a modern democratic political culture. Independents, many of them ex-communists, did extremely well in the local elections in most parts of Hungary. This led some observers, particularly intellectuals in the capital city, to condemn old *apparatchiks* for clinging to power and to rehearse once again the arguments about an anatomised civil society.

However it is possible to take another view of this local society and of the elites who would diagnose atomisation. The leading voices in almost every major party in Hungary in 1990 were agreed that the country needed to proceed rapidly towards a genuine 'market economy' (*piacgazdaság*) and that state interventions and subsidies needed to be curtailed. The Smallholders' Party was progressively isolated in its insistence on a return to the 1947 version of private property landholding, but this nonetheless remained the dominant ideological flavour right across the political spectrum. No wonder that farmers who had experienced the more subtle property relations of the specialist co-operatives were sceptical. They had very good reason to be suspicious of pure market triumphalism, if that implied a withdrawal of state support for small farmers, not to mention the specific subsidies which Tázlár enjoyed because of its unfavourable endowment. Some farmers I talked to were not at all interested in reclaiming the land they or their parents had owned in 1947, believing that even on good-quality land they would hardly earn enough to pay the likely level of land taxes. Many believed that it was vital for the security of the community to preserve the specialist co-operative in its established form, farming its own collective sector as well as continuing to service the farms of its members. The co-operative chairman emphasised again and again the need to give priority to production and to pull together to defend collective achievements. Far from being rejected as a hangover from socialist ideology, this stance won widespread support and admiration.

In other words the recent transition in Tázlár has witnessed a vote of confidence in a number of individuals associated with the *ancien régime*, and in one central institution, the specialist co-operative. It seems to me that this institution is associated not only with existential security for all and substantial prosperity for many, but also with a positively valued public identity and social cohesion. It was the forces associated with the new political parties which seemed to stand for the atomisation of society, for a world of pure market agents in which all farmers would suffer as the state withdrew all its supports, and some would suffer disastrously.[11]

To return now to the arguments of Hankiss, it seems to me that a focus upon the presence or absence of organised interest groups and atuonomous associations is completely inadequate for a diagnosis of the condition of society. In Tázlár not even football provides a very satisfactory basis for public sociability or an enduring local patriotism. The small group of men who gather regularly for scratch matches on the pitch maintained by the co-operative include the village doctor, the former council chairman discussed above, and a number of established entrepreneurs. They are not a very representative group. Most men in these age groups are too busy with other activities: tending their vineyards, seeking out and transporting materials, or getting on with the next phase of their self-help housing. But it would be absurd to present these accumulation strategies as straightforwardly anti-social, for the fact is that men and women combine in groups with kin and neighbours for most of these activities.[12] Within the context of the specialist co-operative, another level of co-operation based upon informal networks deeply embedded in the local community must be taken into account. In other words I am arguing that, far from atrophying in the socialist period, Tázlár continued to develop its own style of social cohesion alongside its remarkable economic transformation, and both were underpinned by the specialist co-operative.

Some readers may doubt the relevance and typicality of this case-study. I do not claim that Tázlár is a very representative community. It was probably unusually low on cohesion in the pre-socialist period, and it has experienced an unusual variant of collectivisation. It might also be argued, with reason, that the theme of 'social cohesion' can hardly be adequately explored in a single small community, and that scale factors should be taken carefully into consideration. In this context it is instructive to look briefly at some developments in Soltvadkert, which has some five times as many inhabitants and is economically much more advanced than Tázlár, for which it serves as a market centre and, increasingly, as a leisure centre. The residents of Soltvadkert seem to spend less of their energy nowadays on accumulation. They have their comfortable houses and their cars, and many have second homes at a nearby resort which is also beginning to attract a few of the new rich in Tázlár. They have lively cinema programmes (including 'drive-in' movies in the summer season) and a flourishing Sports Association, with teams participating in national leagues. But many Soltvadkert citizens spend their leisure time at home, in private ways familiar to most westerners (for example, cable television has enjoyed considerable success in recent years). By 1990, Soltvadkert could also boast a range of clubs and associations far greater than those of Tázlár, from stamp-collectors to pigeon-fanciers. Increasingly these will, I suspect, attract members from the smaller villages of the district.

For me the most interesting example of an interest group in Soltvadkert was the local branch of the Small Tradesmen's Alliance. There was considerable anger in spring 1990, when the Hungarian Democratic Forum (about to become Hungary's main governing party) called a public meeting to re-establish this body under its pre-socialist name 'Craftsmen's Association' (*Ipartestület*) at precisely the same time as the officials of the existing organisation summoned their members to a meeting intended to reach the same goal via an agreed name change. For the Forum activists, such an admission of organic continuity with the socialist period was unacceptable. They wished to see the new Association as a direct successor not to the socialist organisation but to the association dissolved in the late 1940s. However many members did not wish to repudiate the socialist organisation, and they certainly did not wish to risk losing the assets which it had built up. I quote at length from an account which appeared in the local newspaper:

> The Soltvadkert Craftsmen's Association can look back on a distinguished past, and it can claim proudly that it has maintained its identity, even when certain factors dictated that it was not called the Craftsmen's Association, but instead the Small Tradesmen's Alliance. In the past it was precisely this organisation which tried even in the difficult years to draw its members together, to represent their interests as well as conditions permitted, and to offer them protection against attacks from a variety of political currents.
>
> Now, when there is talk of 'renewing the country, unity and democracy, and these are the aims of the governing party, the need for drawing together and unity is greater than ever. That is why we find the initiative of the Hungarian Democratic Forum concerning the establishment of a new Craftsmen's Association incomprehensible.
>
> We ask: shouldn't this question be entrusted to the craftsmen, businessmen and traders themselves to decide? We think they are well able to decide their own fate and future independently, in the interests of their own common goals.
>
> The attendance of members at the two simultaneously convened meetings proved unambiguously which of the two had a quorum. At the Forum meeting there were ten persons at most, whilst the meeting arranged by the craftsmen themselves to renew the association attracted about seventy, that is a majority of those eligible. We were able to hear a serious debate about all the details of the report presented by the representative of the Small Tradesmen's Alliance concerning its proposed evolution into a Craftsmen's Association....[13]

This episode seems to me to exemplify the arrogance of some of those who came along at the end of the socialist period in Hungary to proclaim that everything done in that period was tarnished, and that the only way forward was to start again, or to restore some golden age associated with 1947 (still earlier for many others). That is not at all how many ordinary citizens perceived matters. I cannot prove that Tázlár and Soltvadkert are typical, but I would suggest that the pragmatic style of market socialism which gave rise to the specialist co-operatives was visible in less spectacular ways throughout Kádár's Hungary. The election of a large number of Independents and ex-communists across the country, and perhaps also the very high abstention rates, indicate a failure on the part of the new elites to understand the value attached by many ordinary people to some of the achievements of this particular socialist regime. It is possible to interpret the 1990 electoral results (as Hankiss might) as evidence for the destruction of an earlier civil society and the difficulty in building a new one. But it is worth remembering that a village like Tázlár hardly had even an embryonic civil society before socialism. It became well integrated into the national society and experienced unparalleled material prosperity as a result of reformist socialist policies. Those who believe that the path to a more democratic political future lies in the rejection of gradualist pragmatism (in favour of 'shock therapy' and rush to capitalism in the Polish manner) are pinning their faith in a very naive representation of the Western historical record and an equally naive model of the role of 'the market' in a mature industrial economy. The evidence from Tázlár, and from the grass-roots of a number of other ex-socialist societies, suggests that the preconceptions of the new elites are not widely shared by their citizens.[14] It is easy for intellectuals to sneer about economistic bias, crude consumerism and the political immaturity of the masses, blaming all this on the socialists. But according to normal democratic principles it is surely the new elites who should now be considering their position.

Notes

1. For some typical examples of the 1980s literature about civil society, see Andrew Arato, 'Civil society against the state: Poland 1980–81', *Telos*, No. 50 (Spring 1981) pp. 19–48; Adam Michnik, *Letters from Prison and Other Essays* (Berkeley: University of California Press, 1985); and Timothy Garton Ash, *The Uses of Adversity: Essays on the Fate of Central Europe* (Cambridge: Granta Books, 1989). A more recent

analysis is given by E. Hankiss, *East European Alternatives* (Oxford: Oxford University Press, 1990).

2. For more detail on the 'frontier' conditions which prevailed in this community in the nineteenth century and the poverty experienced by most inhabitants, see Chris Hann, 'A frontier community on the Great Hungarian Plain', *New Hungarian Quarterly*, Vol. 20, No. 74 (1979), pp. 116–22; Hann, *Tazlar: A Village in Hungary* (Cambridge: Cambridge University Press, 1980). See also Ferenc Erdei, *Futohomok (Running Sands)* (Budapest: Athenaeum, 1936).

3. Background on these co-operatives is provided in Janos Gyenis (ed.), *Az Egyszerubb Mezogazdasagi Szovetkezetek (Simpler Forms of Agricultural Co-operative)* (Budapest: Mezogazdasagi/Kossuth, 1971), and in Tibor Simó (ed.), *Szakszovetkezetek Bacs-Kiskun Megyeben (Specialist Co-operatives in Bacs-Kiskun County)* (Kecskemet: Kiskunsagi Mezogazdasagi Szovetkezetek Teruleti Szovetsege, 1987).

4. An excellent sociological discussion of this symbiosis in Hungarian agriculture generally is available in Nigel Swain, *Collective Farms Which Work?* (Cambridge: Cambridge University Press, 1985).

5. This episode is discussed by Nigel Swain, 'The evolution of Hungary's agricultural system since 1967', in Paul Hare *et al.* (eds), *Hungary: A Decade of Economic Reform* (London: Allen & Unwin, 1981) pp. 244–7.

6. I should emphasise that I have not carried out any long-term fieldwork in Tázlár since the 1970s; but I have continued to visit the village regularly, most recently in the summers of 1988 and 1990.

7. See Simó (ed.), *Szakszovetkezetek*, p. 85.

8. He emphasised the difficulty in attracting youth into the public sphere in an article about the Tázlár Culture House in a local newspaper:
    'In recent years people have lost the habit of patronising the Culture House because of more difficult material circumstances and their second jobs, and even third jobs. Our existing groups (zither, drama, puppets, women's club etc.) are working well enough, but the situation of young people cannot be resolved. It is no consolation to know that it's the same everywhere. Howe can we make plans without their participation?' (*Vadkerti Újság*, Vol. 2, No. 5, 1990, p. 14.

9. On Hunting Associations see Imre Szász, *Vadaszat (Hunting)* (Budapest: Szepiroadalmi, 1985) and Arpad Pünkösti, *Az Elithez Tartozni: a teeszelnokok kapcsolatrendszere (To Belong to the Elite: The Networks of Collective Farm Chairmen)* (Budapest: Tomegkommunmikacios Kutatokozpont, 1986).

10. Similar problems concerning rural leadership have also been widely documented in farming co-operatives. See, for example, Peter D. Bell, *Peasants in Socialist Transition: Life in a Collectivized Hungarian Village* (Berekeley: University of California Press, 1984).

11. For further discussion of perceptions of 'markets' in Hungary in 1990, see Chris Hann, 'The transition in Eastern Europe', in Roy Dilley (ed.), *Contesting Markets* (Edinburgh: Edinburgh University Press, 1992).

12. For a fine analysis of such informal networks in rural housebuilding see Endre Sik, 'Reciprocal Exchange of Labour in Hungary', in R.E. Pahl (ed.), *On Work: Historical, Comparative and Theoretical Approaches*

(Oxford: Basil Blackwell, 1988), pp. 527–47.
13. *Vadkerti Újság*, Vol. 2, No. 7 (1990) pp. 7–8.
14. Social anthropologists have begun to play a significant role in documenting the micro-level reactions to the revolutionary changes that have taken place in Eastern Europe. For case-studies broadly confirming the analysis of this chapter see by Peter Skalnik, ' "Socialism is dead' and very much alive in Czecho-Slovakia: political inertia in a Slovak village', in C.M. Hann (ed) *State and Society in Socialist Eurasia*, (London: Routledge); also Tamara Dragadze, 'Land lease and village logic', paper presented at a Georgian Studies Day, University of London, 9 May 1991.

Index